D1135208
Hi!
ANNUAL
1990

I N

Amanda's all alone, without a friend. Read her sad story on ***PAGES 18, 50, 81 AND 106.***

Don't look like that . . . look like THIS . . . on ***PAGE 74.***

Printed and Published in Great Britain by D. C. THOMSON & CO., LTD., 185 Fleet Street, London EC4A 2HS.
ISBN 0-85116-462-5.

I D E

That's all, folks!!

Got long 'n' lovely locks like Claire? ***SEE PAGE 120.***

Fancy a smoochie with Jason? Turn to ***PAGE 123.***

Hi TE

I bet none of you lot believed I was an international megastar — well, now I've got the proof. Some of my admirers have written to me recently — sharing their problems, complimenting me — even asking me out. So, since it's our first annual, I thought I'd share the experience with you.

I've sent them all special goodie bags with poster-size pics of me and a "Hi!" T-shirt, of course!

Lots of love,

Liz x

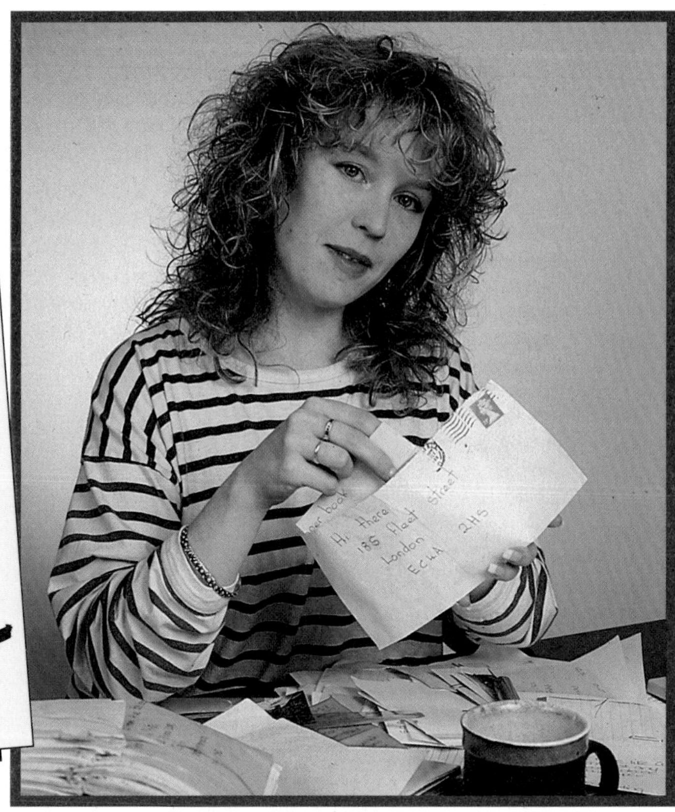

SNIPPE

G'day, cobbers! Just a short note to tell you I love you all and please can I have another number one soon?
Kyles, your favourite Aussie.

No begging on my page, please!

The funniest thing happened to us yesterday. We both smiled and our faces DIDN'T crack!
The Happy Pet Shop Boys.

Do birds bird? Do bees bee? Does a picket fence?
Dave (Moonlighting) Addison.
Pardon?

Hi! Phil here. Did I tell you that I got 5 million fan letters today?
Cutie Phil.
YAWWWN!

Did you know that in the evening our parents don't have to switch lights on? They just ask us to smile!
Five Star.

HERE

At last, I've found you — the answer to my dreams. Ever since I came from my far off planet I've been searching for you. You remind me of the girlfriend I left behind, millions of miles away.

I thought I'd fallen in love once before. She was a Gladiolus, but unfortunately she died (wilted actually) before our true love could really blossom. But now I've found you, I'd like you to come and stay on my far off planet and be my nose-wiper for the rest of our lives.

Well, will you?

Gilbert

At last, I've found someone to love me — a green alien with a runny nose!

Aaargh! I've got a spot!

Joan Collins.

Oh, dear — you'll have to wear your goodie bag on your head then, won't you?

T S

I want to put the facts straight. I am NOT a rough, tough bully who always gets his own way by beating people up. Really, I'm just as gentle as a kitten and as harmless as a fly.

Arnie "Muscles" Schwarzenegger.

PS You'd better print this — or else!

Yikes! You can have the whole page to yourself if you'd like, Mr Schwarzenegger, Sir.

Liz, we've heard all about you in America, so we just had to write. You see, there's this great part up for grabs in our new movie and we thought you'd be perfect for it.

Here's the plot. Tom (Cruise) and Charlie (Sheen) are the goodies in the film and they fall in love with this gorgeous girl (Molly Ringwald) who stays in the next apartment. However, her flat-mate (who's not exactly attractive), takes a fancy to Tom and Charlie and follows them everywhere they go. The film's all about the things they do to try and get rid of her. Like run her over in their car, drop her off the Statue of Liberty and throw her into a cage of lions. Your Ed said you'd be perfect and she'd even let you off work to take part.

Hear from you soon.

The Brats.

Ha! Ha! Very funny!

After three — hands up, wiggle bums, blow a kiss, stick out your tongue, now do a turn. And again. Hands up, wiggle bums, blow a kiss, stick out your tongue, do a turn. Well, Liz, what d'you think of our latest dance routine — isn't it fab?

The Nanas.

But, girls, isn't that the same as every other routine you've ever done? No goodie bags for you three, I'm afraid!

Bubbles and I have been reading "Hi!" ever since it came out and we think it's really great. Bubbles only has one complaint however — he's fed up seeing pin-ups of actors and pop stars (and by the way there haven't been many of me, have there!). He'd like you to include some of his friends in "Hi!". He can introduce you to Mimi, Fifi and Zza Zza, the three nice little poodles from next door. Bubbles is convinced this will boost your sales no end.

For their address write to Bubbles, c/o Michael Jackson, America.

"Hi!" fan, U.S.A.

Er — we'll keep it in mind (I don't think!)

Sniff! Sniff! It's not fair, is it? Everyone says I'm a drip and it's just not true, you know. I work out at least once a month, brush my teeth twice a day and I always fold my clothes neatly and put them away before I go to bed. What am I doing wrong? Why can't I be thought of as a hunk? It really makes me mad when people call me names.

Rick (I'm no wimp) Astley.

Hello again fans! Phil here — amn't I so jolly and full of fun? Don't you just love my cheeky grin? Everyone comments on how great I am at my job. Well I suppose they're right. That's all I have to say really. Can I have a goodie bag?

Your cutie boy next door, Phillip Schofield.

No, you most certainly cannot have a goodie bag — get off my page!

Temptation!

BEST friends Susan and Paula were out shopping—
LOOK, SUSAN, THERE'S A BRILLIANT NEW MOTOWN CASSETTE OUT — I WOULDN'T MIND IT.
PAULA'S DAFT ON MOTOWN. I WISH I COULD BUY HER IT FOR HER BIRTHDAY, BUT IT'S EIGHT POUNDS AND I HAVEN'T GOT ANYTHING LIKE THAT.

I'D BETTER GET HOME NOW. WE'RE HAVING VISITORS TONIGHT.
SEE YOU TOMORROW, THEN. I'VE GOT TO BUY SHAMPOO FOR MUM.

I'LL TAKE THIS TO THE CHECK-OUT. HEY — THAT'S KELLY ARNOLD, AND SHE'S PUTTING SOMETHING INTO HER BAG!

I SAW WHAT YOU DID, KELLY, BUT YOU SHOULDN'T HAVE. STEALING'S WRONG.
Littlewoods Strawberry/Coconut Snowballs
37p 31p
SO WHAT? MY DAD'S ON THE DOLE AND I DON'T GET POCKET MONEY. ANYWAY, THE SECURITY'S SO BAD IN THIS STORE, IT'S DEAD EASY.

BUT YOU'D BETTER NOT TELL ON ME!
I — I WON'T — BUT YOU SHOULD STOP STEALING. IT ISN'T RIGHT.

KELLY'S NOT THE ONLY ONE WHO'S HARD UP. I HAD TO BUY A BIRTHDAY PRESENT FOR GRAN LAST WEEK, SO I'VE ONLY THIS WEEK'S POCKET MONEY TO SPEND ON PAULA'S PRESENT, AND THAT WON'T BUY MUCH . . .

IT LOOKS LIKE I'M GOING TO HAVE TO BUY PAULA SOMETHING CHEAP, BUT SHE ALWAYS GIVES ME REALLY NICE PRESENTS, LIKE THAT RADIO ON MY LAST BIRTHDAY. I WISH I COULD GET HER THAT CASSETTE, BUT THERE'S NO WAY I CAN AFFORD IT, UNLESS . . .

. . . UNLESS I NICKED IT. I'VE NEVER STOLEN ANYTHING BEFORE, BUT I'M DESPERATE, AND KELLY SAYS THE SECURITY IN THE STORE'S BAD — SO IF SHE CAN GET AWAY WITH IT, COULDN'T I?

But soon after—
HOW COULD I EVEN **THINK** OF PINCHING ANYTHING? I MUST BE OFF MY HEAD!

And on Saturday—
I'LL JUST ABOUT MANAGE TO BUY SOME MEASLY SOAP AND TALC FOR PAULA'S BIRTHDAY TOMORROW. I WISH IT COULD BE MORE . . .
HI, SUSAN!

LIKE TO SEE THE WATCH I'VE GOT FOR PAULA?
IT — IT'S REALLY SMART, JENNY.
THAT WATCH MUST HAVE COST A LOT — AND HERE'S ME, PAULA'S BEST FRIEND, BUYING HER SOMETHING CHEAP.

I OWE IT TO PAULA TO GET HER SOMETHING DECENT, SO I'VE MADE UP MY MIND. I **WILL** NICK ONE OF THESE CASSETTES, AFTER ALL.
XXX VISAGE CLUB

THERE'S NOBODY AROUND, SO I'LL SLIP IT INTO MY POCKET, THEN ALL I HAVE TO DO IS KEEP CALM, AND WALK OUT OF THE STORE . . .

But—
EXCUSE ME . . .
OH, NO!
XXX VISAGE CLUB

IS THIS YOUR HAIR-SLIDE, LOVE? IT WAS ON THE FLOOR.
ER YES, THANKS — IT IS.
THANK GOODNESS THAT'S ALL HE WANTED. BUT WHAT IF I **AM** CAUGHT WITH THE TAPE? IT'D BE AWFUL.

27
28
29
I CAN'T DO IT — THERE, THAT'S IT PUT BACK, AND NOBODY'S NOTICED, I HOPE . . .

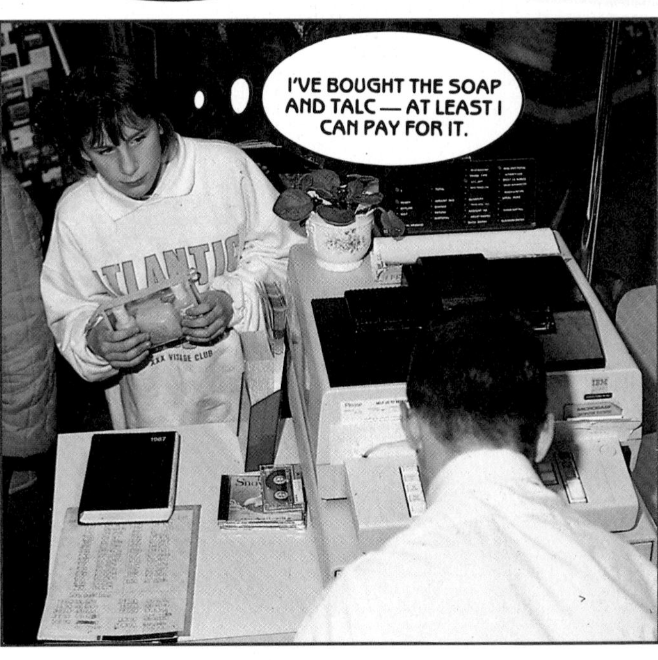
I'VE BOUGHT THE SOAP AND TALC — AT LEAST I CAN PAY FOR IT.

But next day, at Paula's party—
WHAT A LOVELY WATCH, JENNY — THANKS.
PAULA'S HAD A LOT OF BRILLIANT PRESENTS — SHE'S GOING TO THINK I'M REALLY STINGY WHEN SHE OPENS MINE.

But—
SOAP AND TALC — GREAT. IT'S JUST WHAT I NEED.
I'M GLAD YOU LIKE IT, PAULA. I WANTED TO BUY YOU SOMETHING MUCH BETTER THAN THAT, BUT I DIDN'T HAVE THE MONEY.

I KNOW YOU CAN'T AFFORD MUCH, SO STOP WORRYING AND ENJOY YOURSELF.
I WILL, NOW I KNOW THAT PAULA'S HAPPY WITH HER PRESENT.

And next morning—
WHAT'S UP WITH YOU, LISA? AND WHERE'S KELLY?
SOMETHING AWFUL'S HAPPENED. SHE WAS CAUGHT NICKING ON THE WAY TO SCHOOL.

SHE'S IN THE STORE MANAGER'S OFFICE, NOW — AND HER PARENTS HAVE BEEN SENT FOR. POOR KELLY . . .
I'M NOT A BIT SORRY FOR HER. IF YOU DON'T WANT TO BE CAUGHT, YOU DON'T STEAL. IT'S AS SIMPLE AS THAT.

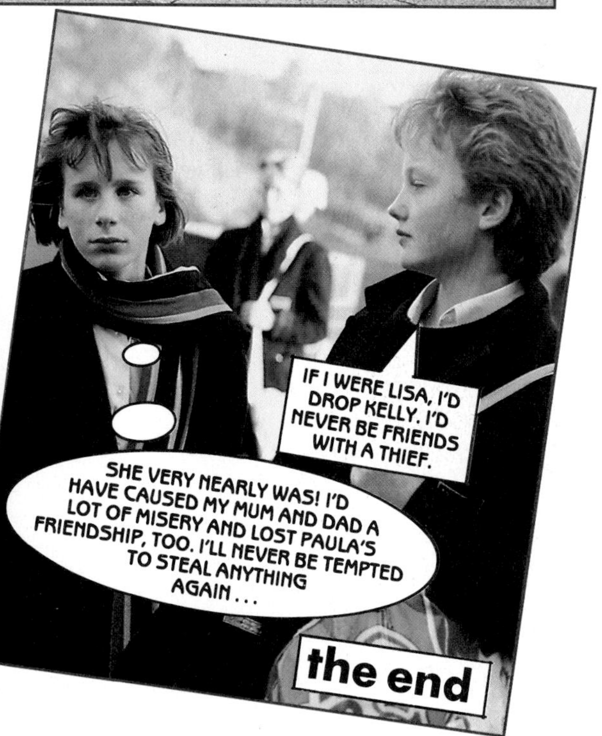
IF I WERE LISA, I'D DROP KELLY. I'D NEVER BE FRIENDS WITH A THIEF.
SHE VERY NEARLY WAS! I'D HAVE CAUSED MY MUM AND DAD A LOT OF MISERY AND LOST PAULA'S FRIENDSHIP, TOO. I'LL NEVER BE TEMPTED TO STEAL ANYTHING AGAIN . . .
the end

BEST FRIENDS AND LOOKIN' GOOD!

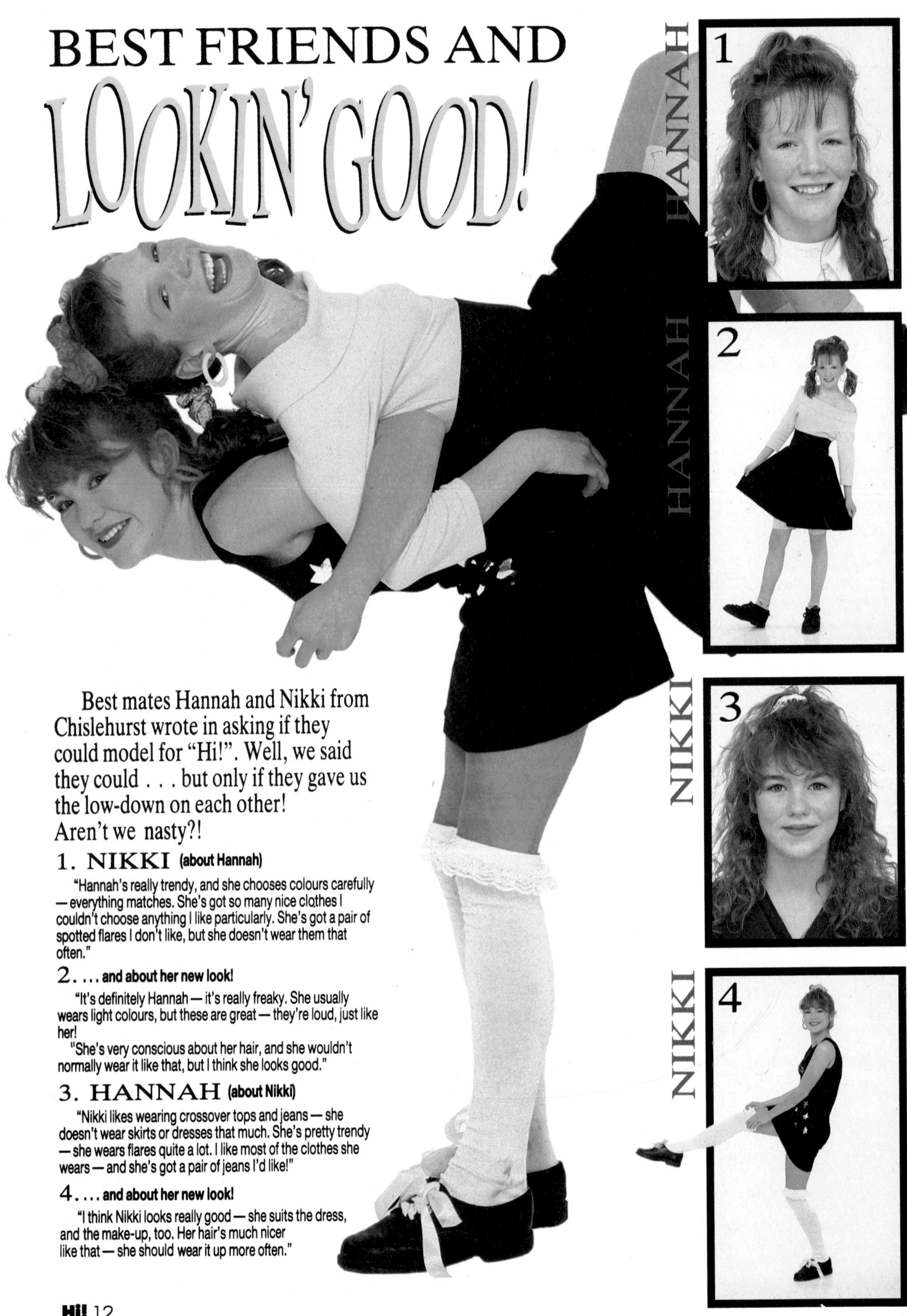

Best mates Hannah and Nikki from Chislehurst wrote in asking if they could model for "Hi!". Well, we said they could . . . but only if they gave us the low-down on each other! Aren't we nasty?!

1. NIKKI (about Hannah)

"Hannah's really trendy, and she chooses colours carefully — everything matches. She's got so many nice clothes I couldn't choose anything I like particularly. She's got a pair of spotted flares I don't like, but she doesn't wear them that often."

2. . . . and about her new look!

"It's definitely Hannah — it's really freaky. She usually wears light colours, but these are great — they're loud, just like her!

"She's very conscious about her hair, and she wouldn't normally wear it like that, but I think she looks good."

3. HANNAH (about Nikki)

"Nikki likes wearing crossover tops and jeans — she doesn't wear skirts or dresses that much. She's pretty trendy — she wears flares quite a lot. I like most of the clothes she wears — and she's got a pair of jeans I'd like!"

4. . . . and about her new look!

"I think Nikki looks really good — she suits the dress, and the make-up, too. Her hair's much nicer like that — she should wear it up more often."

THE RIGHT ADDITIONS

FASHION NEEDN'T COST A FORTUNE. WE TOOK A BASIC OUTFIT AND MADE IT SUITABLE FOR FOUR DIFFERENT OCCASIONS SIMPLY BY ADDING DIFFERENT ACCESSORIES.

BASIC

For starters we used a black jacket, black trousers and a white shirt — clothes everyone should have.

ALL SET FOR SHOPPING

When you go shopping it's essential that your clothes are comfy. We added some chunky ankle boots with bright laces (imagine walking miles in stilettos!) and a bright matching waistcoat. Also essential is a rucksack — for holding your bulging purse and leaving your hands free for carrying all your carrier bags!

THE RIGHT ADDITIONS

A FIRST DATE

First dates can be really nerve-wracking and one of the biggest problems is what to wear — should you be smart or casual? Well, you've got to look as though you've made a bit of an effort, so why not try something like this . . .

. . . to the basic outfit, add a smart waistcoat and some comfy shoes. Again, don't wear shoes with six inch heels — imagine your embarrassment if you keep falling off them. Anyway, he might want to go for a romantic stroll in the park. Also, you don't need to heave a crate of make-up about, so just take a small bag with you for your purse, a comb and a lipstick.

MEETING HIS MUM AND DAD

You've got to remember that all mums like their sons to go out with 'nice' girls and with mums, first impressions count! So, if you turn up in your skin-tight, black mini skirt with trowelled-on make-up and wearing so much jewellery you look like a Christmas tree, chances are you'll make a BAD first impression!

This type of outfit is ideal — it's smart without going over the top. Wear smart shoes that are still easy to walk in and add a nice, girly scarf to brighten it up. Again, just take a small bag — you don't want anyone (especially his mum) tripping over a huge rucksack.

An outfit like this is also suitable for a number of family outings such as tea at Granny's, cousin Linda's wedding and Great Aunt Marjory's 100th birthday party.

A NIGHT ON THE TOWN

This is where you can go a bit OTT. Pile on as much jewellery as you like — providing it all matches, of course. We used gold accessories and matched our model's lipstick to them. You can also wear slightly heavier make-up for the evening, but that still doesn't mean it has to be 3 inches thick! Wear shoes that you'll be able to dance in — there's nothing worse than seeing people dancing about a disco with no shoes on. Add a wide belt to accentuate your waist and take a bag that you can keep with you at all times, as it's all too easy to lose your bag in a disco. Now you're all set to go!

Believe it or not, this lot are called The Jolly Wallies!! Otherwise known as Julie Williams, Nicky Edwards, Mandy Cowburn, Sally Collins, Samantha Board and Tracy de Lobel. What a bunch! They wrote to us just begging to appear in "Hi!" — and how could we resist? So off we popped to Penge!

SIX OF THE BEST!

OKAY — WHERE DID YOU GET THAT NAME?
MANDY: During a P.E. lesson we were trying to find a name for our gang, so we started looking at our initials, and as Julie Williams' initials are J.W. somebody suggested Jolly Wallies, and it just stuck!
SAM: We have to have our initials on our P.E. skirts — that's why we came up with the idea during the P.E. lesson!

DO YOU SEE EACH OTHER OUTSIDE SCHOOL?
NICKY: Yes, we go out quite a lot — shopping and things like that, but most of the time we go round to Julie's house.
MANDY: We watch horror films on her video, although Sally and Nicky get too scared to watch them!

WHAT ABOUT HOBBIES 'N' THINGS?
ALL: We're all daft about animals.
JULIE: We've raised £25 for the RSPCA, £20 for Red Wing Horse Sanctuary and £10 for the World Wildlife fund so far. We've done it through car-washing, raffles and carol-singing.

SO, HAVE YOU GOT ANY PETS? (SILLY QUESTION!)
JULIE: 2 cats, 2 hamsters, a gerbil, a rabbit, a bird and a pond full of fish.
TRACY: 3 dogs, 2 cats, 2 rats and fish.
NICKY: A dog, a rabbit, one goldfish in a bowl, and an aquarium.
SALLY: A kitten called Twiglet!
SAM: A dog, 2 cats, 2 rabbits and a hamster.
MANDY: A dog, a canary, a finch, a goldfish and a hamster.

WHAT D'YOU LIKE MOST ABOUT EACH OTHER?
SALLY: We have great fun and we like mucking about together and generally doing crazy things.
SAM: We like doing impersonations of pop stars like Mel & Kim and Bananarama. We also impersonate some of our teachers, but we don't tell them about that!

WHAT ABOUT, DARE WE SAY IT, FAULTS?!
ALL: Julie's the bossy one!
Tracy puts on an innocent look all the time!
Sam's a bit quiet!
Mandy's a chatterbox!
Nicky worries about everything!
Sally's perfect!!

AND BOYS?
JULIE: Well, we're not really interested in boys.
NICKY: Yes we are!!

DO YOU ALL LIKE THE SAME KIND OF MUSIC?
SALLY: Sort of. Mandy likes Bros and she's really mad about Michael Jackson. Julie likes Jason Donovan and Kylie Minogue. Tracy likes Rock 'n' Roll, especially Elvis! Nicky likes Jason and Kylie as well, and I like Jason and Kylie and Wet Wet Wet.
SAM: And I like Johnny Hates Jazz and Bananarama.

ANY IDEAS WHAT YOU WANT TO BE WHEN YOU LEAVE SCHOOL?
JULIE: I want to work with animals.
MANDY: I want to be a caterer.
SAM: I want to be an architect.
SALLY: I don't know.
NICKY: A secretary or a receptionist in a vet's.
TRACY: I want to be a baker, because I love baking cakes!

DO YOU THINK YOU'LL ALWAYS BE FRIENDS?
ALL: Definitely!!!!!

And from the left . . . Nicky, Sam, Sally, Tracy, Julie and Mandy.

PART 1

Alone!

THE Youth Club had just finished a fundraising campaign —
ISN'T KATHY HERE YET, AMANDA? I DON'T WANT TO ANNOUNCE THE GRAND TOTAL BEFORE SHE ARRIVES.
SHE SHOULDN'T BE LONG, MRS WILMOTT. SHE SAID SHE'D BE HERE BY . . .

PHEW! SORRY I'M LATE, MRS WILMOTT.
THAT'S OKAY, KATHY. NOW, I'D BETTER FIND MY NOTES, SO I DON'T GET THE FIGURES WRONG.
WHERE HAVE YOU BEEN? I WAS GETTING WORRIED.

I WAS TALKING TO MUM. THERE'S SOMETHING GOING ON AND SHE WON'T TELL ME WHAT IT IS.
IS IT ANYTHING TO DO WITH YOUR DAD GOING TO LONDON YESTERDAY?

I THINK SO, BUT MUM SAYS I'VE GOT TO WAIT TILL HE GETS BACK BEFORE . . .

SSSH! MRS WILMOTT'S GOING TO MAKE HER SPEECH.

THE GOOD NEWS IS THAT WE'VE EXCEEDED OUR TARGET BY FIFTY THREE POUNDS. WE OWE A BIG THANK YOU TO THE FUNDRAISING COMMITTEE — ESPECIALLY KATHY AND AMANDA. THEY'RE A WONDERFUL EXAMPLE TO US ALL.

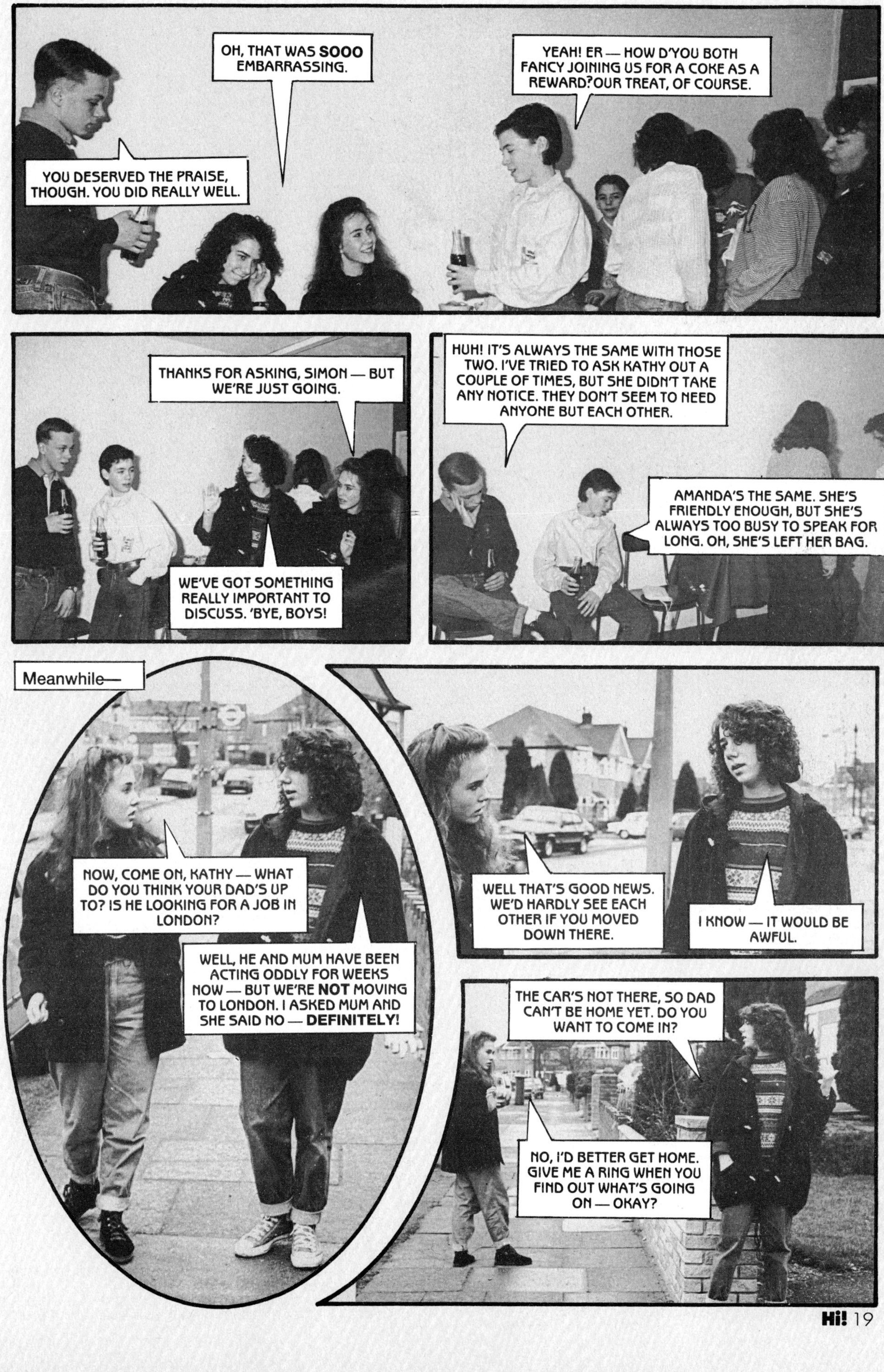

Meanwhile—

NOW, COME ON, KATHY — WHAT DO YOU THINK YOUR DAD'S UP TO? IS HE LOOKING FOR A JOB IN LONDON?

WELL, HE AND MUM HAVE BEEN ACTING ODDLY FOR WEEKS NOW — BUT WE'RE **NOT** MOVING TO LONDON. I ASKED MUM AND SHE SAID NO — **DEFINITELY**!

WELL THAT'S GOOD NEWS. WE'D HARDLY SEE EACH OTHER IF YOU MOVED DOWN THERE.

I KNOW — IT WOULD BE AWFUL.

THE CAR'S NOT THERE, SO DAD CAN'T BE HOME YET. DO YOU WANT TO COME IN?

NO, I'D BETTER GET HOME. GIVE ME A RING WHEN YOU FIND OUT WHAT'S GOING ON — OKAY?

And—
HI, MUM — YOU'LL NEVER GUESS WHAT MRS WILMOTT SAID ABOUT ME AND KATHY?
LET ME GUESS. SHE SAID YOU WERE A GREAT EXAMPLE TO EVERYONE . . .

AW, MUM! HOW DID YOU KNOW?
THAT BOY PHONED. YOU KNOW, SIMON — THE ONE WHO'S **ALWAYS** CALLING! YOU LEFT YOUR BAG AT THE CLUB AND HE'S GOING TO BRING IT ROUND THIS EVENING.

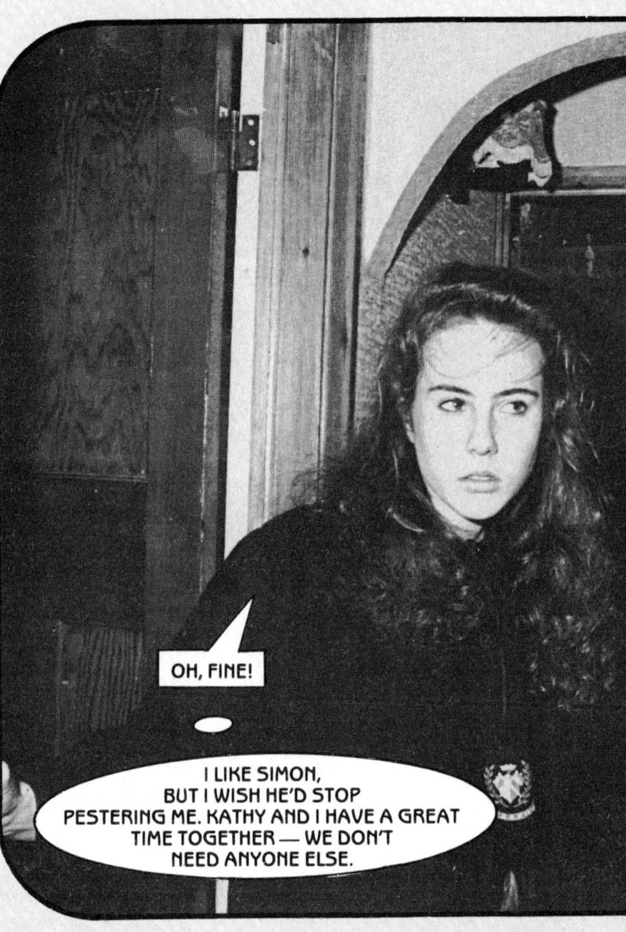
OH, FINE!
I LIKE SIMON, BUT I WISH HE'D STOP PESTERING ME. KATHY AND I HAVE A GREAT TIME TOGETHER — WE DON'T NEED ANYONE ELSE.

Ten minutes later—
KATHY'S DOWNSTAIRS, LOVE. SHE WANTS TO SPEAK TO YOU.
OH, SHE MUST HAVE SOME NEWS. I WONDER WHAT IT IS?

OH, AMANDA — I'VE JUST HAD A LONG TALK WITH MUM AND DAD AND THEY'VE TOLD ME WHAT'S GOING ON. I — I STILL DON'T BELIEVE IT . . .
WHAT IS IT? TELL ME — **QUICKLY!**

DAD'S GOT A JOB IN AUSTRALIA. WE'RE EMIGRATING, AMANDA. WE LEAVE IN FOUR WEEKS!
A-AUSTRALIA? BUT — I . . .

IT'S GOING TO BE AWFUL LEAVING EVERYONE. BUT I'M REALLY EXCITED.
BUT WHAT ABOUT ALL THE PLANS WE MADE FOR THE HOLIDAYS AND THINGS?

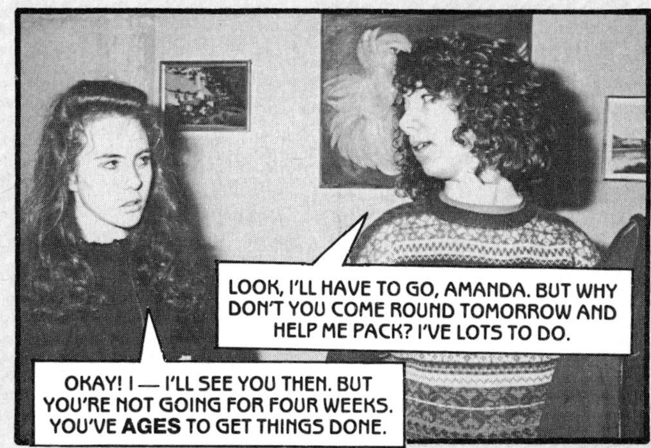

continued on page 50

– WHY WE HATE 'EM!

. . . even the boys we quite like can end up being as 'orrible as all the rest! So why is that? "Hi!" tries to work out just what it is about them that makes us mad!

HE'S asked you out. You've spent hours getting ready, risked life and limb pinching your sister's best outfit, sneaked out wearing the make-up your mum hates you wearing — and he's decided to take you to a football match! Aagh!

He forgot Valentine's Day.

You've spent the WHOLE of the school Christmas disco standing under a sprig of mistletoe, and he hasn't even noticed!

He dumped you for your (ex) best friend!

He never laughs at your jokes.

You've just finished watching the saddest, soppiest film you've ever seen — you're crying your eyes out . . . and he's laughing at you!

It's your first date. You've just met each other as arranged — and he's tried to kiss you already.

You've planned a quiet evening in. Mum, Dad and big sister are all out. There's an ace film on the telly, and a giant pizza heating in the oven. He turns up on time (good) with his best friend in tow (bad).

You're having a coke together in the Wimpy, when his friends appear — with a spare ticket for the Big Match. What does he do? He goes with them!

HIS idea of a great night out is watching stock car racing, followed by a bag of chips.

He's coming to Sunday tea to meet your parents for the first time. He's promised not to wear jeans or DM's, and to wear socks that don't have holes in them . . . then turns up with blue hair!

You're at a disco and he disappears to the loo every time the DJ plays a smoochie record.

It's his birthday. You've spent all your time (and hard-saved-for-cash) searching for exactly the right present for your most favourite person in the whole world.
And what happens when it's YOUR birthday? He buys you a gift token.

You're broke 'cos it's your mum's birthday. There's a film on at the Cannon that you just HAVE to see — and HE'S spent all HIS money on a pair of stupid football boots!

He hates, loathes and detests Bros!

You ask him what he likes about you — and he doesn't know.

Think boys are bad news? They're not really — turn to page 104 to find out some good things about them!

So you don't believe in your stars? Well, you'd be surprised what your stars can

YOUR STAR

ARIES

(THE RAM) Mar 22-Apr 20
Lucky Colour — Scarlet
Jewel — Diamond
Best Days — Tuesday and Thursday
Good Times — Whenever!

How To Spot One
Arians are inclined to have prominent eyebrows and narrow noses. Their skin is often ruddy and they are likely to have moles or marks on their faces. Being the outdoor type they dress for practicality and comfort, but still like to be bright and attractive.

What They're Like
Arian folk are always full of energy and can be very courageous. They're sometimes a bit on the bossy side, though, as they love to be the leader of the pack. These things make them good at team work and selling things. They're good mates but have a very bad temper which is easily sparked off.

Love Life
They're quite possessive so be prepared for jealous outbursts. They get on best with equally forceful people like Sagittarians, Leos and other Arians.

Famous Faces
Some famous Arians are:
Marti Pellow
Keren Woodward
Simon Climie
Nick Berry
Shirlie (Pepsi & Shirlie)

TAURUS

(THE BULL) Apr 21-May 20
Lucky Colour — Any shade of Blue
Jewel — Emerald
Best Days — Monday and Friday
Good Times — October

How To Spot One
Recognisable by their dark hair (often curly), they are usually quite small, but robust and strong. They're pretty graceful, too, with a generous mouth and they often have good singing voices.

What They're Like
Taureans are pretty handy with their dosh — you rarely find a skint one. They're determined — knowing what they want and how to get it and yet they are generally kind, patient and thoughtful. At school they're always hard workers and tend to be good artists and musicians. They also make good nurses and teachers as they are caring and calm in a crisis.

Love Life
They are very dependable and reliable so they won't let you down. They match well with Virgos, Capricorns and other Taureans.

Famous Faces
Some famous Taureans are:
Craig Logan
Bono
Janet Jackson

GEMINI

(THE TWINS) May 21-June 20
Lucky Colours — Yellow, Orange, Green
Jewel — Agate
Best Days — Sunday and Thursday
Good Times — April

How To Spot One
Geminis are usually tall, skinny and pretty athletic girlies. They have nice delicate features and pale skin. Hair can be dark or fair. They also have pretty eyes — blue or grey. Geminis usually choose separates and hate dressing up. They like fun clothes and casual jackets.

What They're Like
They're skilful types, often very clever with it and extremely ingenious and versatile. They love travel, meeting new people learning and are capable of hard work. Although they have difficulty making up their minds and tend to chop and change, once they find what they really want to do they are sure to be successful. They make good actors and performers in general.

Love Life
Librans, Aquarians and other Geminis make a good match with Geminis. They're lively company so you'll never be bored!

Famous Faces
Some famous Geminis are:
Kylie Minogue
Jason Donovan
Prince

CANCER

(THE CRAB) June 22-July 23
Lucky Colours — Green and Grey
Jewel — Ruby

reveal – and not just who you'll be dating next week. Read on and be amazed!

S—AND YOU

Best Days — Thursday and Saturday
Good Times — April and September

How To Spot One
They're generally good looking, of medium height, with strong shoulders and long arms and legs compared to their bodies. They may be slightly plump and are sometimes inclined to scowl. They go for pretty feminine clothes with plenty frills and bows.

What They're Like
Cancer-born girlies are likely to be the most romantic and emotional girls of the zodiac. Your Cancer mate will be a collector and hoarder — so don't open one of her cupboards or you could start an avalanche! They're into antiques and the like and usually get on really well with their grandparents. They can be moody occasionally and hate nothing more than being in the wrong. They're likely to be good at cooking and never have an untidy bedroom — swots!

Love Life
Cancer, the loving sign, seeks a sympathetic and sensitive boyfriend like a Scorpio, Pisces or another Cancer.

Famous Faces
Some famous Cancerians are:
George Michael
Tom Cruise
Mick Jagger

LEO

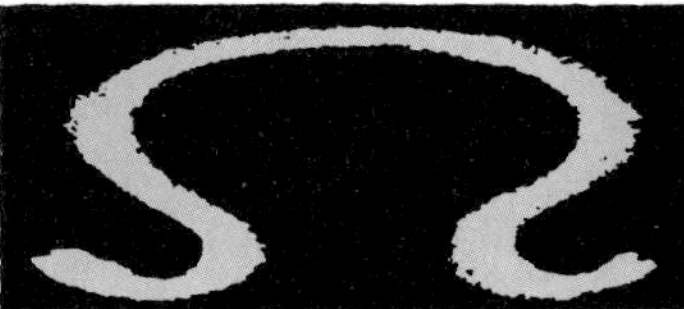

(THE LION) July 24-Aug 22
Lucky Colours — Yellow and Gold
Jewel — Sapphire
Best Days — Wednesday and Thursday
Good Times — March

How To Spot One
Leos are usually well-built types with strong features and ruddy skin. They love wearing the brightest of bright colours and often make the mistake of clashing too many together at once.

What They're Like
Leo is a born leader — proud and determined yet friendly and affectionate. They can't be pushed into doing anything they don't want to by anybody. They're good organisers and can keep their cool in the face of danger (brave girlies). They'll be happiest in jobs where their leadership qualities are used to the full, like community work, management or teaching. They make good team leaders, but like to get their own way. They also give great parties!

Love Life
Friendship and love will most likely be found with Arians and Sagittarians. Watch out though, because Leos are ambitious and get bored easily!

Famous Faces
Some famous Leos are:
Whitney Houston
Madonna
Jacquie O'Sullivan (Bananarama)
Lorraine Pearson (5-Star)

VIRGO

(THE VIRGIN) Aug 23-Sept 22
Lucky Colours — Brown and Grey
Jewel — Sapphire
Best Day — Tuesday
Good Times — July, August

How To Spot One
Folks born under the Virgo sign are usually really skinny with dark hair and pretty faces. They have nice, clear, sparkly eyes. They tend to go for darker colours and are in danger of looking boring sometimes. Most need to accessorise their clothes more.

What They're Like
Virgos are clever shrewd peeps who are down-to-earth and practical. They're perhaps sometimes a bit too cautious and critical. Your Virgo pal won't be a rebel, that's for sure — they like to fit in with the rest. They like precise and accurate work — good treasurers, secretaries and accountants — but watch out, because they're awful gossips and can be fussy eaters too.

Love Life
They're stable, reliable and dependable people who should get on best with Taureans, Capricorns and other Virgos.

Famous Faces
Some famous Virgos are:
Michael Jackson
Carol Decker
Morten Harket
Debbie Gibson

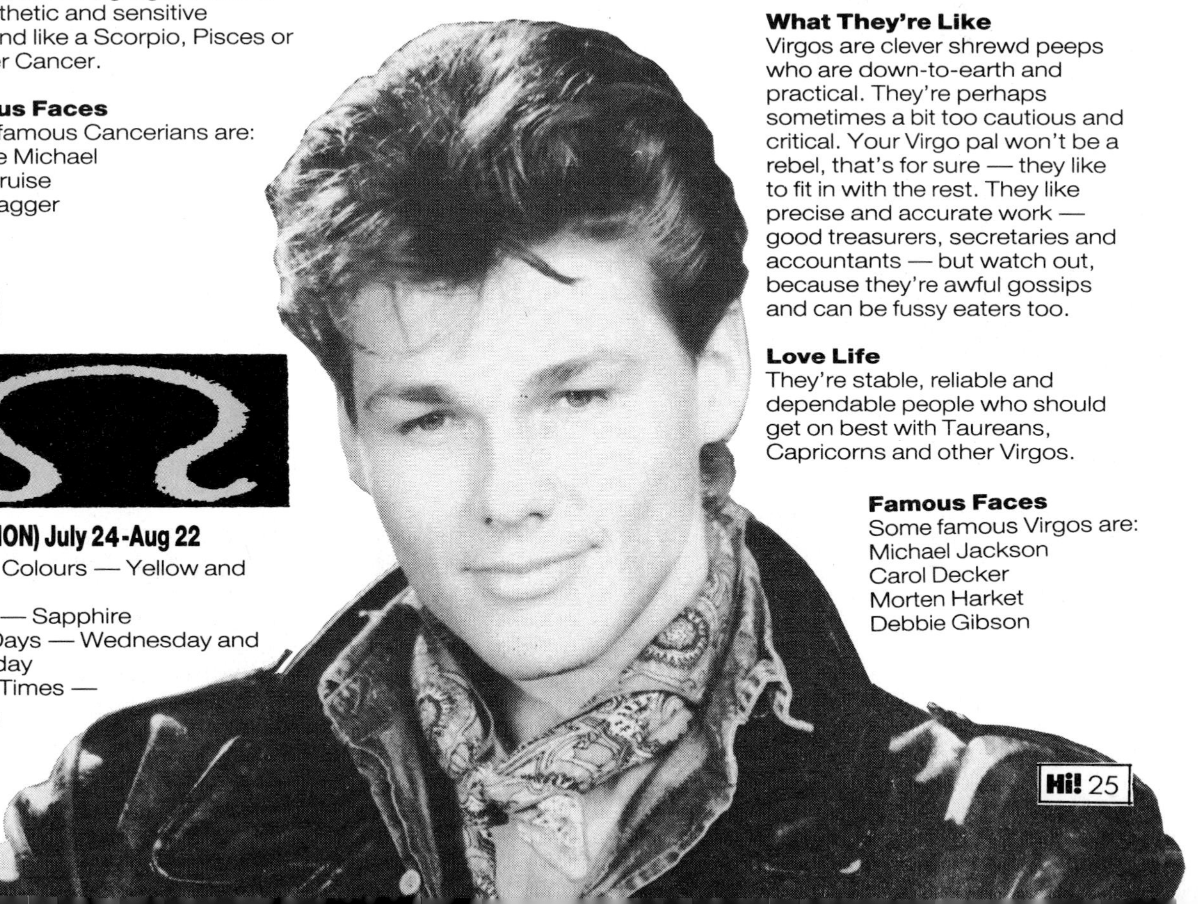

YOUR STARS – AND YOU

LIBRA

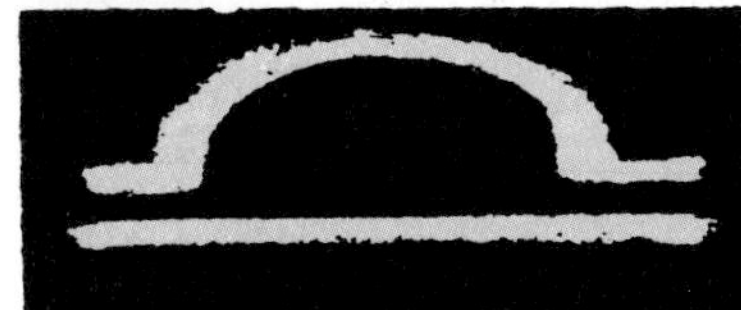

(THE SCALES) Sept 23-Oct 22

Lucky Colours — Green, Blue and Brown
Jewel — Opal
Best Days — Wednesday and Saturday
Good Times — August

How To Spot One

A Libran is often tall, graceful, with fair hair, a dazzling smile and a nice voice. They are prone to having dimples (awww!). They opt for darker clothes with a smart look. They've never a hair out of place.

What They're Like

Librans definitely aren't the tough type so you're unlikely to get into an argument with one. They find it hard to make their minds up so when you ask one a question be prepared for a long wait! They do well in fashion, design or theatre as they have a flair for colour and a good imagination.

Love Life

You'll find they're charming, affectionate and quite romantic but hate being bossed around. They make lively friends and are happiest when among Aquarian, Gemini and Libran friends.

Famous Faces

Some famous Librans are:
Matt and Luke Goss
Bruce Springsteen
Tiffany
Chris Lowe (PSB)

SCORPIO

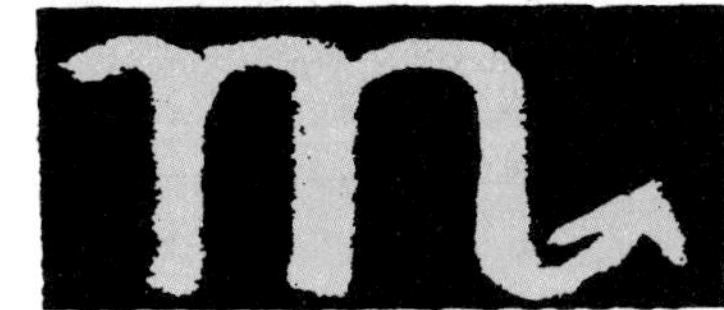

(THE SCORPION) Oct 23-Nov 21

Lucky Colours — Dark Red and Crimson
Jewel —Topaz
Best Day — Wednesday
Good Times — February

How To Spot One

Scorpios are likely to be quite strong people with sharp features — often a prominent nose. They tend to have pale skin. They like dressing up in sophisticated, exotic clothes — especially in bright red — to out-dazzle the rest.

What They're Like

Always with their wits about them, Scorpios can be very shrewd when it comes to getting what they want. They don't suffer fools gladly and once they have their hearts set on something they'll work hard to get it. Scorpios make great scientists, detectives, businessmen, police and doctors. As a friend they may try to dominate you but, on the other hand, they will stick by you through thick and thin. They tend to be bad losers, so avoid board games and the like!

Love Life

You'll be well looked after with a Scorpio as they are protective — almost to the point of smothering you! Good friends will include Pisceans, Cancerians and other Scorpios.

Famous Faces

Some famous Scorpios are:
Prince Charles
Simon Le Bon
Kim Wilde
Mags (A-Ha)

SAGITTARIUS

(THE ARCHER) Nov 22-Dec 21

Lucky Colours — Purple, Mauve
Jewel —Turquoise
Best Day — Friday
Good Times — June, July

How To Spot One

They can be either tall and athletic or have a short, sturdy build. They often have cheery, well shaped faces and a high forehead. Eyes are bright and full of fun. They like clothes that they can move in and they can usually be found in sporty cotton separates — cool and comfy when they're on the go!

What They're Like

Friendly, happy-go-lucky, restless and optimistic — that's the Sagittarian. Although they don't mean it they are always 'putting their feet in it' due to a complete lack of tact! They are honest though and easy to get along with. Outdoor life — camping, hiking and such-like pursuits appeal to Sagittarians. They make great salesmen, and could also do well in advertising and politics! Look out — your Sagittarian pal could be the next P.M.!

Love Life

People who share the Sagittarians love of life are attracted to them — like Arians and Leos.

Famous Faces

Some famous Sagittarians are:
Tina Turner,
Billy Idol,
Walt Disney,
Don Johnson
Sarah Dallin

CAPRICORN

(GOAT) Dec 22-Jan 19

Lucky Colours — Brown and Black
Jewels — Garnet and Ruby
Best Day — Tuesday
Good Times — Mid-June to mid-July

How To Spot One
A Capricorn will most likely be dark haired. Their skin's also dark and usually perfect — 'nuff to make you sick, really! Clothes-wise they tend to stick to darker colours and they aren't dedicated trend-followers.

What They're Like
Your average Capricorn likes a good dollop of tradition and they're very ambitious in a plodding sort of wav. They are hard workers, as well as being practical and honest. All this makes them choose careers in engineering, agriculture, building or banking, so if your Capricorn friend is handy with a spanner and a hoe and seems good with cash — you now know why!

Love Life
A Capricorn will be a faithful chum and is most likely to find true love with Taureans, Virgos and other Capricornians.

Famous Faces
Some famous Capricorns are:
David Glasper (Breathe)
Nathan (Brother Beyond)
Derek B.
Sade.

AQUARIUS

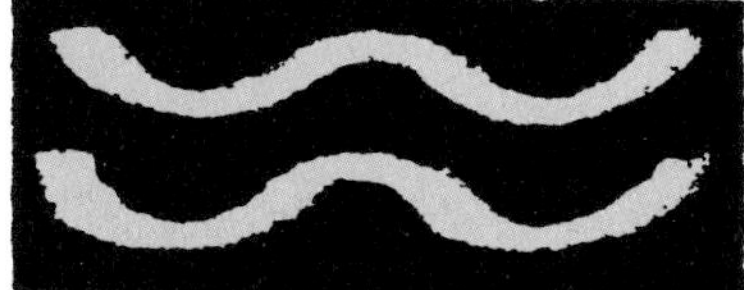

(WATER CARRIER) Jan 20-Feb 18
Lucky Colours — Black and Blue
Jewel — Amethyst
Best Days — Monday and Thursday
Good Times — June, September and October

How To Spot One
Many Aquarians have straight, silky, fair hair with light-coloured eyes and pale skin. They're often tall and slim too. They like to invent their own fashions and have a flair for colour.

What They're Like
They tend to be quiet peeps with sympathetic, kind natures. Underneath this though, are very strong willed girlies who know their own minds! This makes them jolly good at being bosses and important people because they're good at handling stress and pressure.

Love Life
Aquarians love love and indeed, love to be loved. Their ideal matches are Geminis, Librans and other Aquarians.

Famous Faces
Some famous Aquarians are:
James Dean
Phil Collins
Mozart

PISCES

(THE FISH) Feb 19-Mar 20
Lucky Colours — Blue, Purple, Mauve
Jewel — Bloodstone
Best Days — Tuesday and Saturday
Good Times — January, March

How To Spot One
Your Pisces pals will probably be quite small but pretty. They may have lovely eyes and nice soft skin. They're always tidily and smartly dressed but hate to be uncomfortable. They tend to hate high heels and are always found in flatties!

What They're Like
They tend to have heaps of imagination but this makes them prone to daydreaming. They're really likeable, though, and find it easy to make friends. They shun routine, preferring to come and go as they please. Maths is not a strong point with Pisceans but they do make good doctors, chefs and archaeologists, believe it or not!

Love Life
Pisceans are genuine and sincere folk and they would do anything for their loved one — who is likely to be a Scorpio, Cancer or another Piscean.

Famous Faces
Some famous Pisceans are:
Jon Bon Jovi
Patsy Kensit
Bruce Willis

PROBLEM PROFILE

THE CHRISTMAS BLUES

Christmas comes but once a year — thank goodness! It always promises to be such a happy, cheerful time, but for some people it doesn't always work out this way. Christmas can be one of the most upsetting times as well as one of the happiest.

Here's what Carol from Droylesden has to say . . .

"Why am I always so depressed at Christmas time? I'm never happy with the presents I receive — no matter how many I get. I'm sure I must make Christmas day miserable for the rest of my family because I just can't join in and have fun."

There's so much hype surrounding Christmas that we expect the whole occasion to be one long party with hundreds of gifts — a cosy, comfy world of Santa Claus and tinsel. Unfortunately, usually we find it just ISN'T like that and the whole day ends up as a real damp squib. Christmas won't be really successful unless you try to make it so. Instead of just thinking of yourself try to make Christmas a special time for others. By choosing gifts carefully for relatives and friends you may find that you actually get more pleasure watching their delight than actually thinking about how many presents, etc. you got yourself.

"You always read in magazines like 'Hi!' that Christmas is such a great time," says a Michael J. Fox fan from Hereford. **"Everyone's going to parties and discos, but what about me? I never go anywhere at Christmas or hear of any parties. How come I always miss out?"**

Sometimes you have to work hard at Christmas to make it as much fun as possible. Don't sit around waiting for other people to organise parties — why not do it yourself? Parents are usually quite amiable at this time of year and a party would certainly give you something to look forward to.

Caroline from Surrey says,

"I really dread Christmas 'cause my nan comes to stay and she's a real pain! I can't do anything while she's around — she just ruins the whole thing for me. How can I persuade my mum and dad not to invite her along?"

Christmas is a time for families and it's not very nice to leave relatives out — especially if they are alone. Try to be tolerant of other people's feelings. Make visitors feel welcome — don't treat them as if they are ruining your Christmas. If you make them feel welcome they may relax and enjoy themselves too.

Fiona from Edinburgh has another worry at Christmas.

"I never have much money to spend on presents and I feel so mean. I only get £1 a week for pocket money and that doesn't leave me much extra money to save. It makes me feel really miserable when I can't buy nice things for my friends."

Unless you can put a limit on how much you will spend at Christmas, it's easy to go on spending and spending. Gifts don't have to cost a lot — why not make special presents for parents and grandparents? I'm sure they'd appreciate it much more.

"Why does Christmas always end up as one enormous BORE?" asks Lisa from London. **"I'm fed up of relatives coming round, everyone stuffing their faces, then falling asleep on chairs! How can I make Christmas more fun?"**

Why not plan a special Christmas day for your family? Think of games you can all take part in — nothing too complicated, something like charades, perhaps? Or why not help Mum to prepare the Christmas meal — that way you'll be so busy the day will fly by and you'll be so tired you'll be content to sit down and watch telly in the evening!

The most noticeable feature of the letters I've received about Christmas is that most of you just EXPECT Christmas to be a wonderful occasion. You don't seem to realise the hard work which goes on behind the scenes to try to make it a special day for you.

Maybe if YOU put in a bit more effort, you'd get more reward on the day. Make this year's resolution to have a fun Christmas 1990. Why not take part in a pantomime, organise a disco or a party? Go on — get some Christmas spirit!

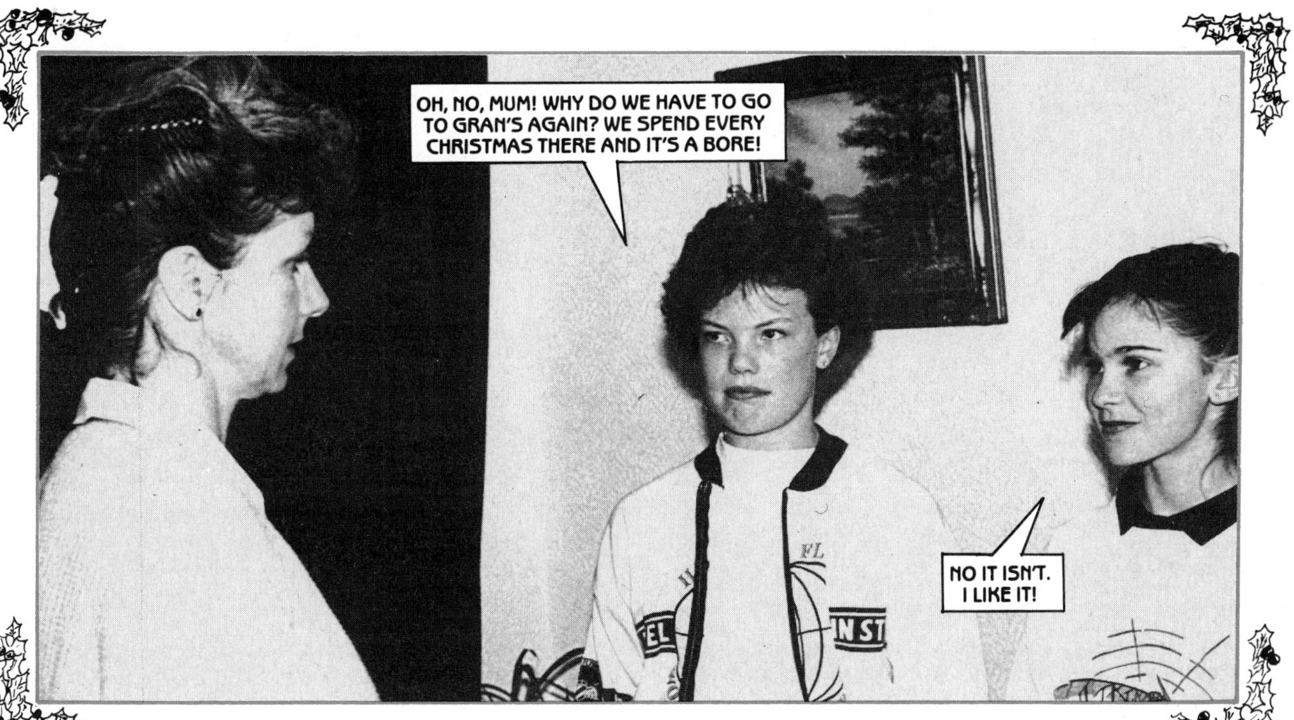

LONELY THIS CHRISTMAS

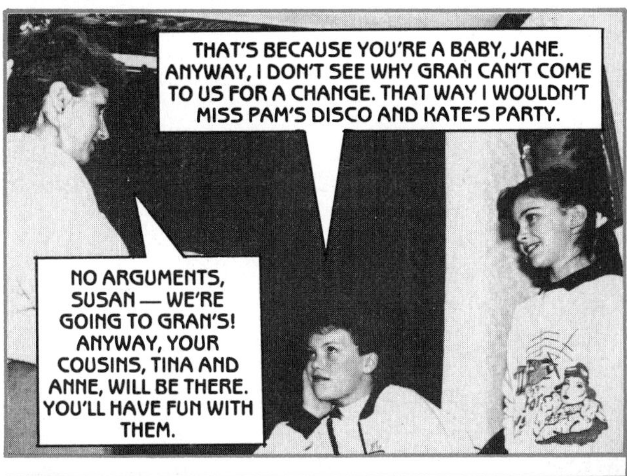

THERE MUST BE **SOME** WAY I CAN GET OUT OF THIS. I SUPPOSE I COULD PRETEND TO BE SICK . . . NO, I'VE GOT IT! IF ONE OF MY FRIENDS INVITED ME TO STAY, MUM **COULDN'T** REFUSE TO LET ME GO!

So—
POOR YOU! CHRISTMAS AT YOUR GRAN'S SOUNDS REAL BORESVILLE.
THAT'S WHY I HOPED I COULD STAY WITH YOU. IF YOUR MUM PHONED TO ASK, I'M **SURE** MY MUM WOULD AGREE.

OH, BUT DIDN'T I TELL YOU? WE'RE GOING TO SPAIN FOR CHRISTMAS THIS YEAR. DAD'S DECIDED HE WANTS TO TRY TURKEY IN THE SUN FOR A CHANGE.
LUCKY YOU. THAT SOUNDS GREAT!
BUT IT'S LOUSY FOR ME. MAYBE I'LL HAVE MORE LUCK WITH NICKI.

But—
SORRY, SUSAN, MUM SAYS WE CAN'T SQUEEZE IN ANYBODY ELSE. WE'VE GOT RELATIVES COMING TO STAY THIS CHRISTMAS.
OH, WELL. THANKS FOR ASKING ANYWAY, NICKI.

I'LL THINK ABOUT YOU ENJOYING ALL THE PARTIES WHILE I'M STUCK IN THE BACK OF BEYOND.
POOR YOU. I'M REALLY SORRY I COULDN'T HELP.
NOT HALF AS SORRY AS I AM.

So, two days before Christmas—
THAT'S US THEN. COME ON, SUSAN. WE WANT TO GET THERE BEFORE LUNCH.
BORESVILLE, HERE I COME!

I HOPE SUSAN DOESN'T SPOIL THE HOLIDAY FOR EVERYONE. I THINK I'M GOING TO HAVE TO DO SOMETHING ABOUT THIS.

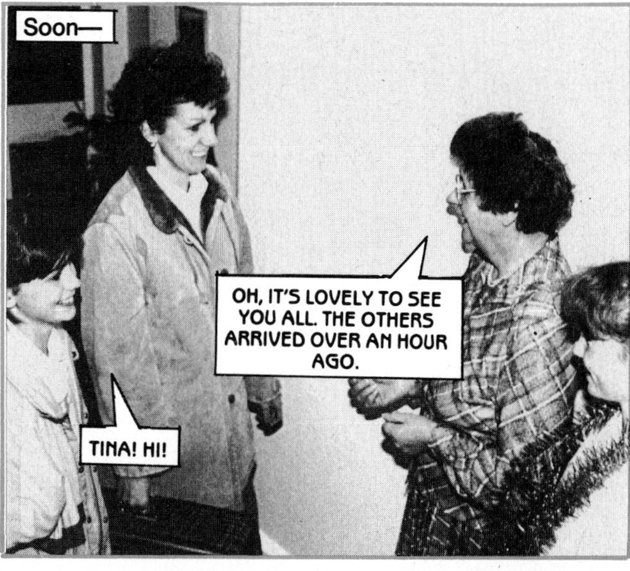
Soon—
OH, IT'S LOVELY TO SEE YOU ALL. THE OTHERS ARRIVED OVER AN HOUR AGO.
TINA! HI!

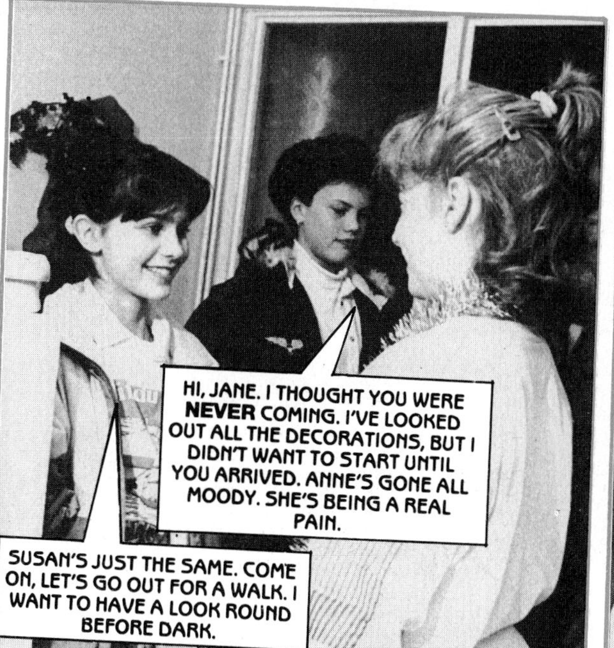
HI, JANE. I THOUGHT YOU WERE **NEVER** COMING. I'VE LOOKED OUT ALL THE DECORATIONS, BUT I DIDN'T WANT TO START UNTIL YOU ARRIVED. ANNE'S GONE ALL MOODY. SHE'S BEING A REAL PAIN.
SUSAN'S JUST THE SAME. COME ON, LET'S GO OUT FOR A WALK. I WANT TO HAVE A LOOK ROUND BEFORE DARK.

And, later—
HI, ANNE. COMING TO HELP US?
NO WAY.
YOU TWO LOOK DAFT ENOUGH AS IT IS. YOU'RE NOT GETTING US INVOLVED.

VISITORS FOR YOU, GIRLS. IT'S ALEX AND HIS FRIEND, JOHN.
OH, WHAT DO **THEY** WANT?
HI, GIRLS. WE'RE ON THE LOOK-OUT FOR A COUPLE OF WORKERS AND YOU TWO LOOK JUST RIGHT.
OH! HI, ALEX.
WOW! HE'S REALLY CHANGED:

YOU'RE LOOKING GOOD, SUSAN. YOU'VE CHANGED SINCE LAST YEAR.
SO HAVE YOU! YOU LOOK MUCH TRENDIER FOR A START. AND WHAT'S ALL THIS ABOUT A DISCO TONIGHT?

SO YOU'LL COME TO THE YOUTH CLUB TO HELP US DECORATE THE HALL FOR TONIGHT'S DISCO?
OF COURSE! THAT'S ALL PART OF THE FUN OF CHRISTMAS.

I DON'T BELIEVE I HEARD THOSE REMARKS.
ME NEITHER. BUT AT LEAST THEY'RE HAPPY. I'M GLAD WE BUMPED INTO ALEX AND JOHN WHEN WE WERE OUT. IT LOOKS LIKE WE'LL HAVE A HAPPY CHRISTMAS NOW, AFTER ALL.
OH! ARE THE DECORATIONS FINISHED?
NOT QUITE — BUT WE THOUGHT WE'D LEAVE IT TO THE EXPERTS.
BESIDES, MUM, WE'VE GOT SOME REALLY IMPORTANT DECORATING TO DO.

WE'VE GOT TO DECORATE OURSELVES FOR TONIGHT'S DISCO. WE WANT OUR SHARE OF CHRISTMAS ROMANCE.
YEAH! MIND YOU, WITH OUR NATURAL CHARM AND GOOD LOOKS THERE'S REALLY ONLY ONE THING WE NEED . . .

. . . MISTLETOE! THINK IT'LL BE USEFUL?
I HOPE SO, JANE. I CERTAINLY HOPE SO!
the end

NIGHT AND DAY

We gave three "Hi!" readers two looks to see them through the day . . . and into the night — so they're ready for any occasion! Perhaps you'll pick up a few tips, too!

1. For an everyday look, make-up artist Susie kept Rosanne's make-up light and natural. Rosanne's skin is fairly pale, so Susie applied a light base, with just a hint of peach blusher. A peachy-pink lipstick was used on her lips. Rosanne's eyes were highlighted with pale brown.

"It's really nice and I like my hair, it seems quite easy to do."

2. Creamy, red lips give Rosanne an evening look — just right for a disco or party. More blusher was added to her cheeks, and a touch of yellow to her brow to complete the look.

"I really like this — it's my favourite. I don't think I could do my hair like this myself, though — it looks too difficult. And I love the lipstick colour — it really suits me."

1

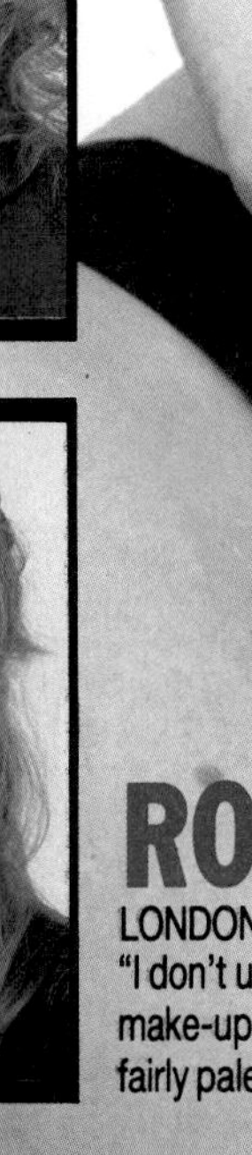

2

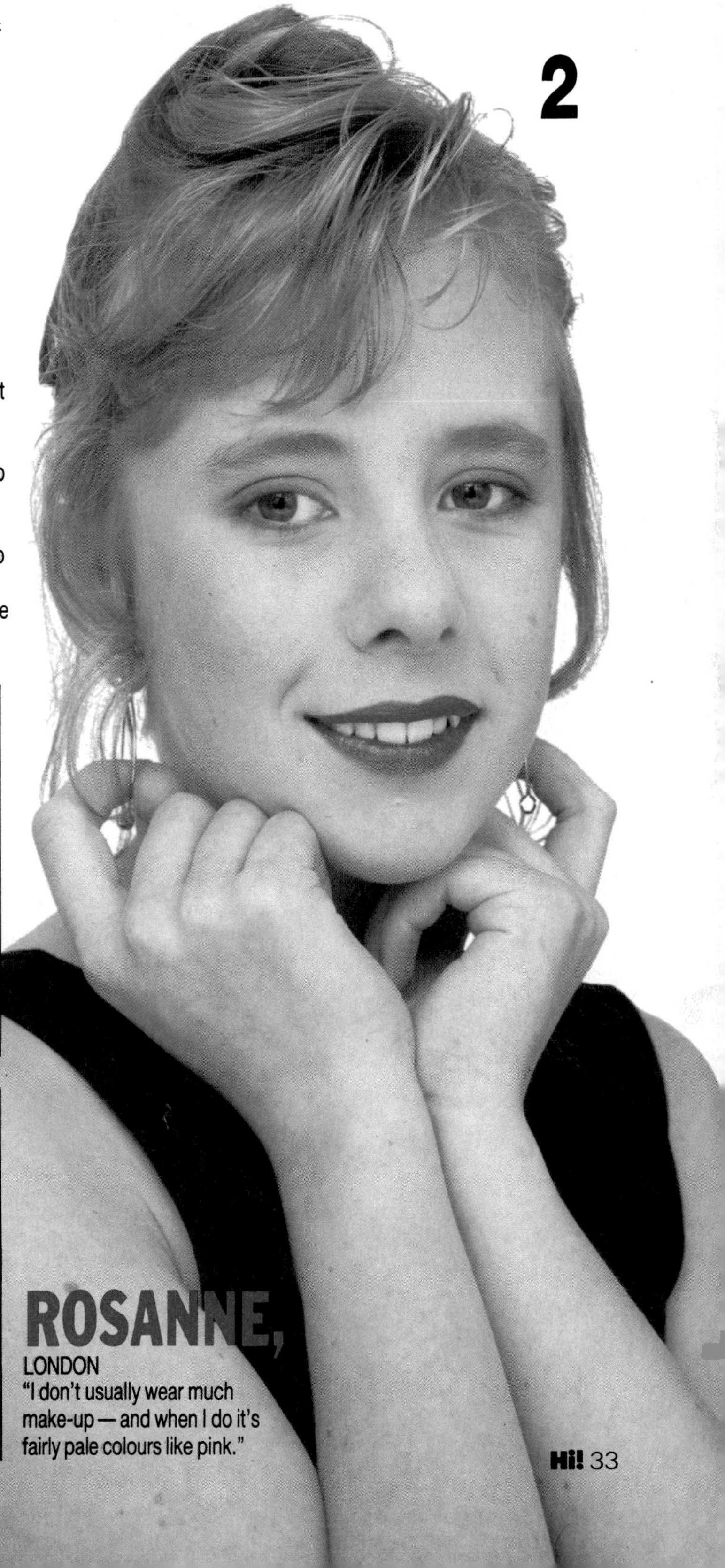

ROSANNE,

LONDON

"I don't usually wear much make-up — and when I do it's fairly pale colours like pink."

c

VICKI, "I'd quite like to be a model,
LEWES but I need some ideas on how to style my hair and some hints on how to put on make-up."

1. Vicki has thick, straight hair, with a fringe she's trying to grow out. Susie curled up the ends of her hair with a hot brush, and gently sprayed back the fringe to keep it in place.

A soft yellow-gold was brushed over the lids, with a hint of brown added at the corners of the eyes. A matt pink was used for the lips.

"I love my hair — I like the way it turns up, and it seems easy to do. Susie used a lip brush to apply the lipstick, which I've never done — I learned a lot."

2. Vicki has always wanted curls, so that's what she got! Susie used Clairol Benders to add some bounce to Vicki's hair, then added a bright green scarf to add some colour.

Green was added to her lids, and her lip colour was changed to bright pink for this party look.

"I like my curls — I expected them to be tighter than this, but they're great. I wouldn't have chosen such a strong lip colour, but I like it."

2

.REBECCA'S THE WINNER OF THE 1989 "Hi!" COVER GIRL COMPETITION!

1

REBECCA, "I had my perm done a few months ago, but I don't seem to be able to do much with it. I don't wear make-up very often, so it'll be interesting to see what I look like."

1. Susie scrunched some mousse through Rebecca's hair to define the curls, then let it dry. Rebecca's fringe tended to hide her face a little, so Susie pinned it back.

Pale brown shadow and soft pink lips kept Rebecca's day look natural, with a hint of pink on her cheeks to give her a touch of colour.

"My make-up's subtle, but nice."

2. For an evening look, Susie decided to pin back Rebecca's hair to the side, leaving a few bits straggling round the back and on top. Spray made sure the hair stayed in place — gel was used to define the curls.

Pink was used on the brows and lips — and now Rebecca's ready for anything!

"I think my hair's lovely — it's like something out of 'Dallas' — really nice for going out. I'd normally wear brown on my eyes, but I like the pink."

2

1

2

3

4

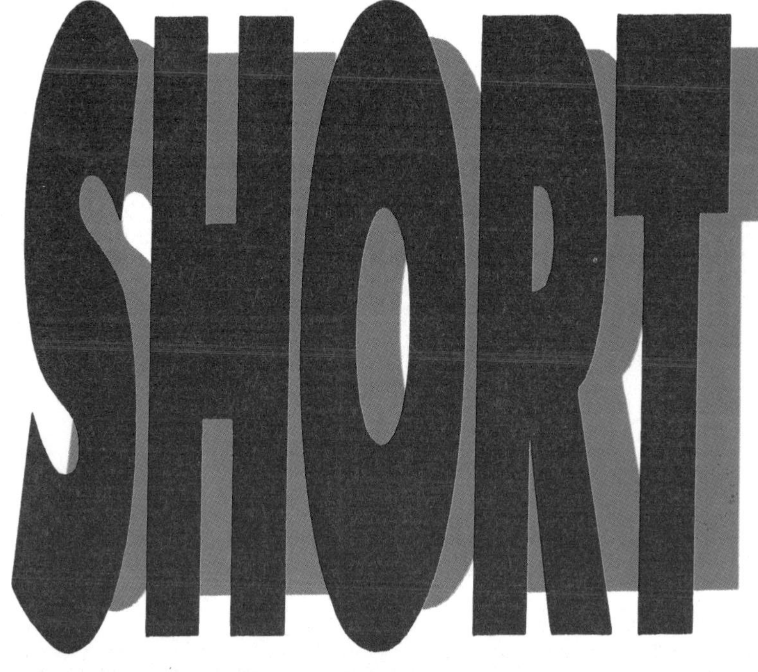

SHORT 'N' SWEET

Got short hair and can't do a thing with it? Well, don't be stuck — check out these short 'n' snappy styles.

1.
Our model, Kezia, has a short bob which is cropped into her neck at the back, and although it looks great already, it sometimes gets a bit boring.

2.
This is a really easy style. All you have to do is slick one side of your hair back with some gel and pull three small strands down for some detail. The other side is just brushed through to tidy it up.

3.
To achieve this style first work some mousse through your wet hair. Now tip your head upside down and push your hair upwards and forwards as you dry it. When your hair is dry you can backcomb any stray bits into place. Finish off with a quick squirt of hairspray (ozone friendly, of course!) to make sure it stays put.

4.
If your hair looks like a haystack and you can't get it under control then slick it back with some wax. Simply work the wax through your hair, pull down one strand at the front and shape it into a curl to soften the look slightly.
When you want to wash the wax out, put your shampoo on BEFORE you wet your hair. This will help to dissolve the grease and make it easier to wash out.

THE INCREDIBLE HUNKS–

WHY WE LOVE THEM SOOO MUCH!

They're absolutely gorgeous, and we go weak at the sight of them . . . but why? "Hi!" tries to find out just what makes these incredible hunks so hunky!

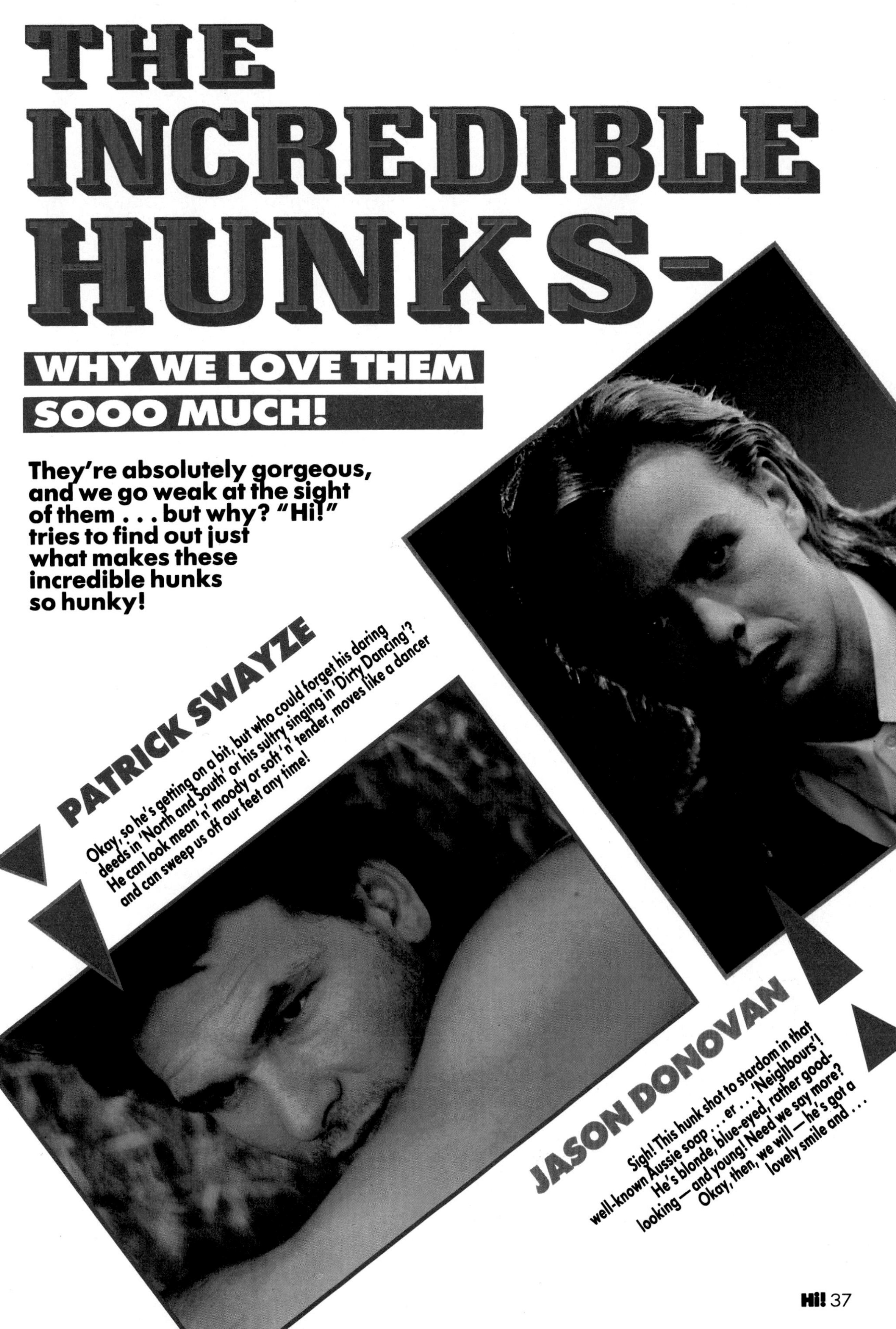

PATRICK SWAYZE

Okay, so he's getting on a bit, but who could forget his daring deeds in 'North and South' or his sultry singing in 'Dirty Dancing'? He can look mean 'n' moody or soft 'n' tender, moves like a dancer and can sweep us off our feet any time!

JASON DONOVAN

Sigh! This hunk shot to stardom in that well-known Aussie soap . . . er . . . 'Neighbours'! He's blonde, blue-eyed, rather good-looking — and young! Need we say more? Okay, then, we will — he's got a lovely smile and . . .

MATT GOSS

MORTEN HARKET

One of the hunkiest blokes to come out of Norway is Morten (well, probably the only one, actually!). Morten looks lots of fun, and doesn't mind sending himself up occasionally—his cheeky grin has won him loads of fans.

GEORGE MICHAEL

He seems to have been around for yonks, but improves with age! He writes brill songs, and although he might not look so hunky underneath the stubble, George's rugged looks are okay by us.

PHILLIP SCHOFIELD

You only need to hear Bros boy Matt sing to know why he makes us girlies go all a-tremble. Remember last Crimbo's swoonsome hit 'Silent Night'? Ooh! With that voice and those looks . . . well, it's no wonder Matt's a hit!

RIVER PHOENIX

River looks as if he likes to be alone . . . he always seems to be thinking about something—or someone. And don't you wish it was you? It's his air of mystery that makes River so romantic—that, and the fact that he looks so good!

MICHAEL J. FOX

Is Michael too short to be a hunk? "Hi!" doesn't think so! It's been a few years since Mikey hit our TV screens in 'Family Ties', and he doesn't seem to have gotten much older since then—but that's why we like him! He looks like he could be the boy next door . . . and don't we wish he was!

Everyone's favourite TV and radio presenter—that's Phil! Ever since he first appeared on Children's BBC, he's been a big hit with viewers, and it's no wonder! He looks good, has a twinkle in his eye that would make anyone swoon, and a smile that means fun!

RICK ASTLEY

Okay, maybe 'hunk' isn't the right word for Rick, but who could resist this songster? We reckon Rick's a bit of a smoothie, and that's part of his attraction—he looks like he would know just how to look after you. Aah . . .

FACE I

SHAPE UP

ROUND FACE — To slim down chubby cheeks, brush some shaper (use a shade slightly deeper than you would normally use as blusher) under your cheekbones. What cheekbones? Well, to find them, smile at yourself in a mirror and see where your cheeks lift. Brush the shaper just under that area, taking the colour right out to your hairline. Don't use too much colour, though — the idea is to create a soft shadow, not end up with two brown stripes like a Red Indian! Then take a paler blusher along your cheekbones. If you've got a slight double chin, dust some shaper just underneath.

LONG FACE — The idea is to shorten and widen the face, so brush blusher on to your cheekbones, not underneath, and fade it out towards the hairline. Then put shaper on to the point of your chin. This shortens the face. But make sure you don't put the shaper on to the front of your chin — this'll make your face look even longer! Highlighter brushed on to your cheeks above the blusher will do two things — emphasise the bones and add width.

SQUARE FACE — A square face needs softening, so take shaper from under the cheekbones right down to the jaw line. Don't go mad, though — you don't want to look like you need a good wash! Keep it soft and light. Then brush highlighter on to your cheekbones to widen the upper part of your face.

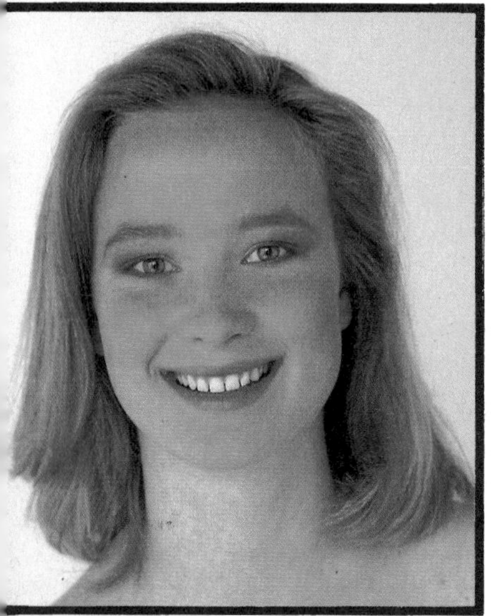

IMPORTANT!

Don't try all this out just before a v. special date or the disco of the year. It takes a bit of practice to get it right, so try it out at home when you're going nowhere, then get a good mate to tell you what she thinks!

FACTS

GOT chubby cheeks, piggy eyes or a chin like Desperate Dan? Don't panic! Here's how to change the shape of your face by using make-up. 'Seasy when you know how!

EYES RIGHT

DEEP SET — Apply pale shadow over the lid, taking it to just above the hollow. Then on the bone between the lid and the brow brush on a slightly darker shade. Highlight just under the brow with a very pale shade. Finish it off by smudging a kohl pencil below the lower lashes. ▶

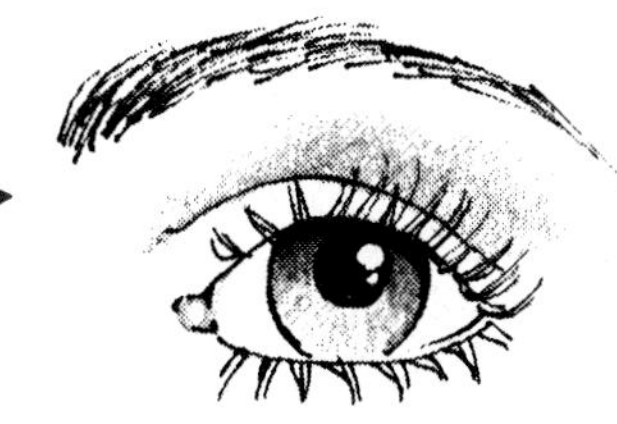

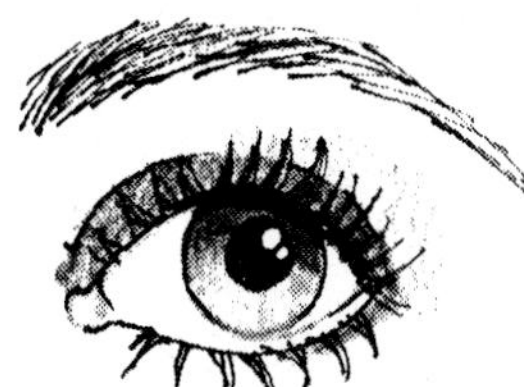

◀ **PROMINENT** — Cover the lid with a deep matt shadow, curving out just under the bottom corner of the eye. Use a pink tone just underneath the brow. Eyeliner makes the lid look smaller, so smudge kohl pencil softly along top lashes and below bottom lashes.

SMALL — Apply a strong shadow around eye, leaving inside corner free. Build the shadow out at the sides, but only take a little underneath. Use a paler shade in the corner, taking it up and under brow as well. ▶

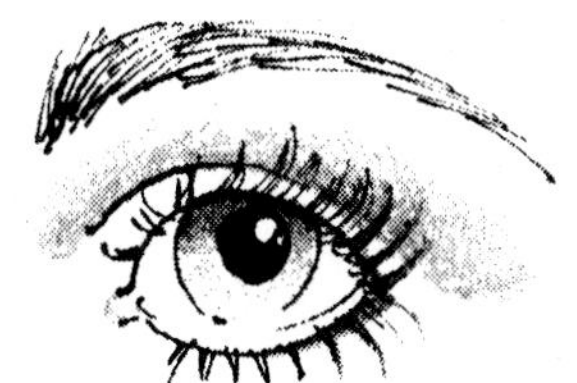

◀ **ROUND** — Shading should be kept light. Cover the whole lid with a pale shade, then take a deeper tone and fill in the socket area, extending at the corners parallel to the eyebrows. Outline with smudgy kohl, extending the lines slightly at the edges.

DROOPY — Uplift is needed at the outer corners, so extend the shadow outwards and upwards until it almost touches the browline. Blend a pale shadow under the eyebrow. Draw in a socket line, smudging well so that the effect is soft. Use kohl pencil from the centre of upper lashes and raise it slightly at outer edges. ▶

LIP SERVICE

TOO THIN — Again outline with a lightish pencil, but this time just outside the natural lip line. Stop a little short at the corners, then fill in with a deeper tone.

TOO BIG — Outline with a pencil just inside the natural line, using a lightish shade, then fill in with a slightly deeper shade.

UNEVEN — When lips don't match in thickness, use two different shades — a dark one for the thicker lip and a lighter one for the other.

BE NOSEY

TOO LONG — Use a shader slightly darker than you would normally wear as a blusher and brush some on to the tip of your nose.

BROAD — Using a shader, shade the sides from the eyebrows to the nostrils.

WIDE BRIDGE — To slim the bridge of your nose, take a fine brush and a creamy foundation about three shades lighter than your skin tone. Draw small triangles at the inner end of your eyebrows. Make sure you blend this in well!

WIDE NOSTRILS — Using a thin brush and pale creamy foundation, draw a triangle on either side of the nostrils and again blend very carefully.

LAST WORD

If you've got an oval face, big eyes, luscious lips and a slim nose, then you can wear just about any make-up you want . . . and we just hate you! AAARGH!

jill's proble

Each week a lot of my mail concerns the same type of problems — boys, parents and school. I try to give the answers which I think will help, but sometimes it's not enough to put your minds at ease. So I thought it was time I spoke to the experts — our readers themselves! I dropped in on a sports session at Linlathen school and spoke to some girls who all play basketball together. Here's what they had to say about some of the problems YOU may worry about.

boyfriends

Lots of my letters ask how to get a boyfriend. Is that because there is a lot of pressure on girls who don't have boyfriends?
Everyone: "No, definitely not!"
Pamela: "I don't think any girls should go out with someone just so they can say they have a boyfriend."
All the girls agreed that they didn't feel it was necessary to have boyfriends. None of their friends made fun of them — 'cos most of them didn't have a boyfriend either!
Would their parents mind if they DID have a boyfriend?
Ashley: "My mum says bring him home for tea one night if you're going out with somebody."
Debbie: "My parents don't mind as long as I tell them who the boy is."
None of the girls felt they had to go out with boys behind their parents' backs. Most parents seem happy to allow their daughters to go out with boys — as long as they get a chance to meet them first. This should make lots of you feel more confident about talking to your parents about boys instead of worrying how they will react. You'll usually find that most parents CAN be reasonable if you talk to them first — BEFORE you jump to conclusions.

kissing

—Yes, the dreaded word! Most of you seem to turn into crumbling wrecks at the very thought of it. Here's what the girls had to say.
Angela: "The first time I kissed a boy I was a bit nervous — I didn't know if I was doing it properly! It turned out all right, though!"
Ashley: "My first boyfriend showed me how to kiss!"
Have any of you NOT been able to kiss a boy?
Everyone: "No!"
Kissing is a bit daunting at first, but it DOES come naturally to everyone. Even if there is a clash of teeth on the first attempt it doesn't mean you were doing it all wrong — you'll soon get it absolutely right.
So, how do you know if a boy fancies you?
Everyone: "He follows you around and keeps staring at you!"
Donna: "He blows you kisses!" (I think she was joking about this!)
What do you do if you fancy him too?
Debbie: "I'd just go right up to him and ask him to go out with me. If he says no, just say all right then and forget him."
"I'd get my best friend to go up and ask him."
Angie: "No, boys like you to approach them yourself."
Now maybe you'll believe that it IS possible to make the first move — even if you have to get your friend to do it for you. Boys CAN be shy too, you know. If you're going to hang around and wait for THEM to ask you out you may have to wait for a long time!

parents

We all have little arguments with parents, but somehow as we get older these little arguments tend to grow in size. Do the girls agree?
Debbie: "Yes, as you get older it's harder to get on with them. It's because you're growing up and your body is changing. Whatever's going on inside you makes you feel touchy and easily upset.

"In a way it's easier for us to argue with our parents because we know that they love us and will still support us after it's all over."

What do most arguments with parents revolve around?
Ashley: "Not getting to stay out late and not being allowed to go where you want to."
Everyone: "They make you do things you don't want to do and don't let you do the things you do want to do!"
However, after saying that, all of the girls agreed that their parents were quite lenient and understood what was going on.
Yvonne: "There's not much I wouldn't talk to my parents about."

school

Often I answer girls' problems by advising them to talk to a trusted teacher. How did the girls feel about this advice?
Everyone: "We'd NEVER go to a teacher with our problems!"
They all said they'd either talk to a relative or a close friend. However, I still think that in lots of cases a teacher is a good person to turn to for help — especially if your problem is connected to school.
Something which worries lots of girls is that they'll lose their friends when they go to secondary school.
Angela: "You do lose lots of friends, but you also meet new people."
Ashley: "It's almost like moving house."
So what do you do if you find that a new girl is forcing her way into your twosome?
Debbie: "I'd find a new friend or give my friend a choice — me or the new girl. I'd try not to stop talking to my friend though."
Good advice from Debbie because it is difficult to keep friends when you go to a new school. Everyone's finding new friends who they get on with. It's best not to fall out with people because of this — don't worry, you'll find new friends, too.

Thanks to the girls from Linlathen — I hope their advice helps you to get over some of your problems.
If you still find something bothering you, though — don't hesitate to write to me at our usual address.

model

Models have to wear all sorts of styles of clothes whethe
what they REALLY think! We asked three of our favourit
for "Hi!" and what type of clothes they like to wear whe

WHAT do you like about the clothes you've chosen?

I like clothes that are comfy and hard wearing and I have a lot of things that I can mix and match. I'm not too keen on chain store fashions — they all look the same to me — and I buy a lot of second-hand stuff. In fact, my granny gave me this jacket and it's my favourite.

WHAT about the clothes you model for "Hi!"

They're not too bad. This outfit's not what I'd choose for myself, but I don't hate it. Although I must admit these stripy tights are a bit wild for me!

WHY do you like this outfit?

Well, I like simple, uncluttered clothes and I wear a lot of black. I think that trousers this style are very flattering, and although they look casual just now, I can also wear them for a night out with some different accessories.

AND what do you think of these clothes?

I didn't like the clothes I modelled for "Hi!" to start with — I thought they were really girly. But I've liked a lot more recently and I would wear this. It's much more my style and the jacket's lovely.

clothes

hey like them or not, but we were curious to find out
nodels what they thought of the clothes they modelled
hey can do the choosing!

WHY is this your favourite outfit?

I think it's quite versatile — I can wear it to a disco or for something like going out with my mum and dad. These trousers are really comfy because the elastic waistband expands and I can pig out as much as I like without them cutting me in two! Also, if I want a more casual look I can wear the trousers with flat shoes and a black jacket.

AND do you like the clothes for "Hi!"?

Yes, I do. I haven't really modelled anything yet that I've hated. I'd wear most of the things that I model for "Hi!" and, in fact, I have a coat just like this one!

CRING

WE'VE ALL HAD THAT PRESENT, HAVEN'T WE? THE ONE THAT YOU SMILE SWEETLY AND SAY FOR—BUT REALLY HATE.GRANNIES, AUNTIES AND FRIENDS READ NO FURTHER!

JENNI SMITH, 11 AND JENNY DOUGLAS, 12.

JENNI — "The worse present I've ever had was a pair of socks that I got from my gran. They were pink and had horrible flowers on them."

JENNY — "I once got these burgundy slippers. They had a heel on them and everything. YUK!!"

CRINGE!

WENDY PETERS, 14.

"The worse present I ever got was from my friend. It was a set of plastic bead necklaces in all sorts of colours like beige, pink and green. I just about died when I opened the package, but I pretended to like them."

CRINGE!

LORRAINE GIBB, 12.

"I always get things like talc and bubble bath. I hate getting those packs, you know, the ones with talc, foam bath, bath cubes and a sponge. And even worse is when you get 300 pairs of knickers!"

KIRSTY SCOTT, 15.
SUZANNE PETERS, 15.
RHIAN JOHN, 15.

SUZANNE — "The worst present I could be given would be a Bros poster."

KIRSTY — "Or anything out of the women's department in Marks & Spencer."

RHIAN — "You always get lots of writing paper — boring. I got a filofax once — it was gross!"

SUZANNE — "The best thing about Christmas is mistletoe! I'd like to kiss Dolph Lundgren under it."

RHIAN — "No, James Dean!"

KIRSTY — "Or Charlie Sheen!" Girls! Girls!

CRINGE!

AUDREY, 15.

"I don't know what got into my mum, but last year she gave me a Barry Manilow LP! She put the album inside the cover of a Harry Secombe album, so I suppose in a way I was a bit relieved when I pulled out the LP and found it was actually Barry Manilow not Harry Secombe!"

JOHN BLACK, 15 AND BILLY BOYD, 15.

JOHN — "You always get slippers at Christmas. One year I got a pair that looked like they were elf shoes!"

BILLY — "Socks! Grey, green, blue, every colour you can think of! I always get them."

CRINGE!

LORRAINE ROBERTSON, 13 AND YOLANDE SMART, 13.

LORRAINE — "Green slippers have got to be the worst present I've ever received. They were really plain and boring! I mean GREEN slippers!"

YOLANDE — "Mine's worse than yours! I was given a flowery nightie from one of my great aunties!"

YOU KNOW THANK YOU PARENTS

AMY LOCKART, 13.

"When I was about nine I got a pack of knickers — with a day of the week printed on each one!"

LIZ (AGE UNKNOWN!)

"This present totally ruined my Christmas. My brother dropped loads of hints that he was going to get a personal stereo for my Christmas! I was excited 'cos it was what I really wanted! On the big day I opened my parcels and sure enough there was a box which had a picture of a personal stereo on the lid. Unfortunately, inside there were two tea-towels! I also got a mop and bucket for my flat! Very exciting — boy was I mad at my brother!"

WE RECKON THERE ARE A FEW THINGS SOME RATHER FAMOUS PEOPLE WOULD *HATE* TO GET.

BRUCE WILLIS —
A wig! Even though we know he's going bald, he wouldn't like to admit it.

JOAN COLLINS —
Another facelift! One more and we're sure she'd be talking through her navel!

MICHAEL J. FOX
A leading lady who's over 5 ft. He's a bit small is our Mikey.

TIFFANY —
A floaty Laura Ashley frock. She just doesn't like those girly clothes, does she?

Hi!
JASON DONOVAN

SUCCESS OR FAILURE

Which is in store for you? Try our fun quiz to find out. But be honest — the conclusions may not be quite what you expect!!!

1. You're being allowed to choose the next family holiday. Where will you go?

a) Anywhere there's lots of fun, nosh and boys, boys, *boys!*
b) The place you went last year. It was great.
c) Somewhere you could combine culture with sun — like Italy.

2. How did you fare in your last exams?

c) Very well. You always do.
a) Not *too* badly — considering you didn't study.
b) So-so. The same as usual.

3. You're about to go out when Dad says you're wearing too much make-up. How would you react?

b) Take a little off. You can always re-apply it later.
c) You seldom wear make-up, so it isn't likely to happen.
a) Call him an old-fashioned prat and storm out anyway.

4. You're offered a small part in the school play. Would you . . .

a) Burst into tears? You wanted the lead.
c) Accept — on condition rehearsals don't interfere with your schoolwork.
b) Start learning your lines?

5. Which career do you fancy most?

c) Teacher or accountant.
b) You don't know yet. You'll decide in a couple of years.
a) Pop star or actress. *Definitely.*

6. What's your ideal way to spend an evening?

a) Bopping at the local disco or roller skating or . . .
b) At the cinema watching the latest Brat Pack movie.
c) Reading — anything from War and Peace to the back of the cornflakes packet.

7. You really fancy a boy at school. How would you get him to notice you?

b) Write a note and get a friend to pass it on.
c) You wouldn't bother. Boys aren't very important to you at the moment.
a) Walk up to him and ask him for a date. No point being shy, is there?

8. Mum wants to go to a Chinese restaurant, Dad fancies Italian, but you've a craving for a curry at the local Indian. Would you . . .

a) Scream and stamp your feet until you got your own way?
c) Suggest you draw lots?
b) Let Mum and Dad fight it out? You don't *really* mind where you go.

9. And finally, if the "Hi!" Ed. gave you £50 to spend, what would you do with it?

c) Put most in the bank and buy yourself a treat with the rest.
a) Blow it — on all the things Mum won't buy for you.
b) You'd have to think about it.

CONCLUSIONS

MOSTLY A

You're selfish, bad tempered and lazy! If you call that being a success, fine, but it won't pay in the long run, you know. On the plus side you DO seem to have a lot of confidence and a sense of fun, but unless you change your ways and start being a little more understanding, you could find yourself without any friends to have fun with.

MOSTLY B

It's easy to sum up your chances of being a success. At the moment they're nil/zilch/zero!!! You're quite happy to plod along doing the same old thing all the time, aren't you? And when was the last time you argued — about ANYTHING? Come on, give yourself a shake and stand up for yourself — before you're totally swallowed up by the crowd.

MOSTLY C

If your aim is to be a prim little bore — then you're sure to be a first class success. You're too sensible to be true! You COULD be a success at almost anything, 'cause you're obviously intelligent and have a mind of your own, but you need to loosen up a bit and have fun while you're young. If you're not careful, you could reach forty before you're fourteen.

MIXTURE OF ALL 3

Yippee! Success at last! You're well-balanced — a nice mixture of good sense and fun! What more could anyone ask for? You'll probably go on to be a big success, whatever you choose to do. But remember, success has got to be worked at, it doesn't just drop into your lap. Keep on your toes and make sure your big chances don't pass you by.

Alone!

PART 2

continued from page 21

SORRY, BUT I'M TOO BUSY. YOU'LL HAVE TO FIND SOMEONE ELSE.
I SEE . . .
I'M NOT BUSY AT ALL, BUT IF I LET JIM IN, HE'LL START TALKING ABOUT KATHY — AND SHE'S THE LAST PERSON I WANT TO TALK ABOUT.

IT'S BEEN THREE WEEKS SINCE SHE LEFT, BUT I HAVEN'T EVEN HAD A POSTCARD FROM HER. SHE CAN'T HAVE FORGOTTEN ABOUT ME ALREADY, CAN SHE?

Later, Amanda walked past Kathy's old house —
OH! FOR A MOMENT I THOUGHT KATHY AND HER FAMILY HAD COME BACK — BUT IT'S NOT THEM. IT MUST BE THE NEW PEOPLE MOVING IN. I WONDER IF MUM KNOWS ANYTHING ABOUT THEM?

THEY HAVE A DAUGHTER CALLED FIONA WHO'S NEARLY THE SAME AGE AS YOU. WHY DON'T YOU OFFER TO SHOW HER ROUND TOWN?
I — I SUPPOSE I COULD . . .
I CAN READ MUM LIKE A BOOK. SHE HOPES I'LL MAKE FRIENDS WITH THIS GIRL, AND FORGET ABOUT KATHY.

Next morning —
MUM! IT'S A LETTER FROM KATHY AT LAST!

SHE SAYS SHE'S HAVING A GREAT TIME, AND SHE'S MADE LOTS OF NEW FRIENDS. SHE'S SORRY SHE DIDN'T WRITE SOONER BUT SHE DIDN'T HAVE TIME.
SLOW DOWN! SLOW DOWN! I CAN'T TAKE IT ALL IN AT ONCE.

Amanda read the letter again, then —
I MISS HER SO MUCH, BUT SHE DOESN'T SEEM TO FEEL THE SAME. ALL SHE WRITES ABOUT IS THE FUN SHE'S HAVING.
I'M SURE SHE IS MISSING YOU, LOVE, BUT SHE'S GOT THE SENSE TO GET ON WITH HER NEW LIFE. THAT'S WHAT YOU SHOULD DO, TOO.

MAYBE YOU'RE RIGHT — BUT I DON'T KNOW WHERE TO START.
HOW ABOUT SAYING HELLO TO THE NEW GIRL — FIONA? YOU NEVER KNOW, YOU COULD GET ON REALLY WELL.

AW, MUM. I CAN'T JUST WALK UP TO HER HOUSE. I WOULDN'T KNOW WHAT TO SAY.
I WAS TALKING TO HER MUM YESTERDAY AND SHE TOLD ME FIONA WANTED TO GO TO THE YOUTH CLUB. IF YOU ARRANGE THINGS, I'LL GIVE YOU A LIFT THIS EVENING AND WE CAN PICK FIONA UP ON THE WAY.

So —

SORRY I KEPT YOU WAITING, AMANDA. I JUST COULDN'T MAKE UP MY MIND WHAT TO WEAR.
THAT'S OKAY. WE HAVEN'T BEEN WAITING LONG.
YOU'D THINK SHE WAS GOING TO A NIGHTCLUB, NOT THE YOUTH CLUB.

WHAT'S THE TALENT LIKE AT THIS YOUTH CLUB? I HAVEN'T MET ANY BOYS SINCE I GOT HERE.
TALENT? WELL, I DON'T KNOW. IT'S ALL RIGHT, I SUPPOSE.

And —

HI, EVERYONE — THIS IS FIONA.
HI! ANY CHANCE OF A GAME OF DARTS? I'M NOT VERY GOOD, BUT I'M SURE ONE OF YOU LADS CAN HELP ME.
SURE — YOU CAN PLAY A MIXED DOUBLES MATCH WITH ME. I'M SIMON, BY THE WAY.

SIMON DIDN'T EVEN LOOK AT ME. I MUST HAVE KNOCKED HIM BACK ONCE TOO OFTEN.
HI, AMANDA. I DON'T SUPPOSE YOU'VE HEARD FROM KATHY YET?
HMM? OH — YEAH, SHE'S HAVING A GREAT TIME. SHE SAID SHE WAS GOING TO WRITE TO YOU, BUT YOU MIGHT HAVE TO WAIT A WHILE.

continued on page 81

MEGA-BIG QUIZ

A

Unjumble these letters to find five albums and name the artists who recorded them.

1. SUHP
2. NWRITONA
3. SCODI
4. SURCIC
5. TAWEND

B

Name the lead singers of these groups and tell us how old they are.

1. Brother Beyond
2. Wet Wet Wet
3. Climie Fisher
4. Duran Duran
5. Simply Red

C

Some really difficult questions — if you get all these right you're brilliant!

1. **Simple Minds had a No. 1 hit about a child that came from where?**
2. **Name a worldwide, seasonal EP from Erasure. (Bet you don't get this one!)**
3. **He sang about a Smooth Criminal.**
4. **Who was she driving crazy in January?**
5. **Whose album contains these songs and what's it called? She Wants To Dance With Me, Hold Me In Your Arms and Take Me To Your Heart.**
6. **Where was Debbie Gibson lost?**
7. **Name Kylie Minogue's *second* single release.**
8. **Can you name the two presenters who got it all wrong at the last Brit Awards?**
9. **Can you name the Christmas No. 1's for 1987 and 1988 and who sang them?**
10. **Who was riding on a Love Train?**

Look for lots of Neighbours and some of their favourite places in this wordsearch.

DAPHNE
DES
JAMIE
MIKE
BOUNCER
MADGE
HENRY
CHARLENE
SCOTT
HAROLD
JIM
PAUL
HELEN
GAIL
ROSEMARY
BEVERLEY
JULIE
ROB LEWIS
MRS MANGEL
JANE
LUCY
LASSITERS
WATERHOLE
RAMSAY STREET
ERRINSBOROUGH
COFFEE SHOP

N E L R A L H C H A R L E M Y
X D A P H A W H A R O L D R E
E L S O D S E A T O P V E S L
H R A X O S M R T S I R S M R
Y U R S L I A L E E T N S A E
W A T I S T D E A M R E U N V
D E C R N I G N M A P H N G E
L H L O O S T E S R O T O E B
U W E B M B B E X Y C U L L T
A C U L O A L O R I L U J I E
P A U E E R N E R S M A Y A E
J O S W O N L G J O M W R G R
I O H I C J A M I E U X N Y T
N T N S G A P A M A D G E R S
A P P S E N L N A M E G H C Y
D A P H N E D A P H N O O E A
I H O J A N F L I M P T O P S
T E I L U J U F O R T E K I M
C H I L R E N I O S O R T E A
X E R O M B O U N C E R U D R

ANSWERS

A

1. PUSH : Bros
2. RAINTOWN : Deacon Blue
3. DISCO : Pet Shop Boys
4. CIRCUS : Erasure
5. WANTED : Yazz

B

1. Nathan Moore
2. Marti Pellow
3. Simon Climie
4. Simon le Bon
5. Mick Hucknall

We were only joking about the ages — we don't know either!

C

1. Belfast.
2. Crackers International EP
3. Michael Jackson
4. Fine Young Cannibals
5. Rick Astley, Hold Me In Your Arms
6. In Your Eyes
7. The Locomotion
8. Samantha Fox and Mick Fleetwood.
9. 1987, Pet Shop Boys: Always On My Mind 1988, Cliff Richard: Mistletoe and Wine
10. Holly Johnson

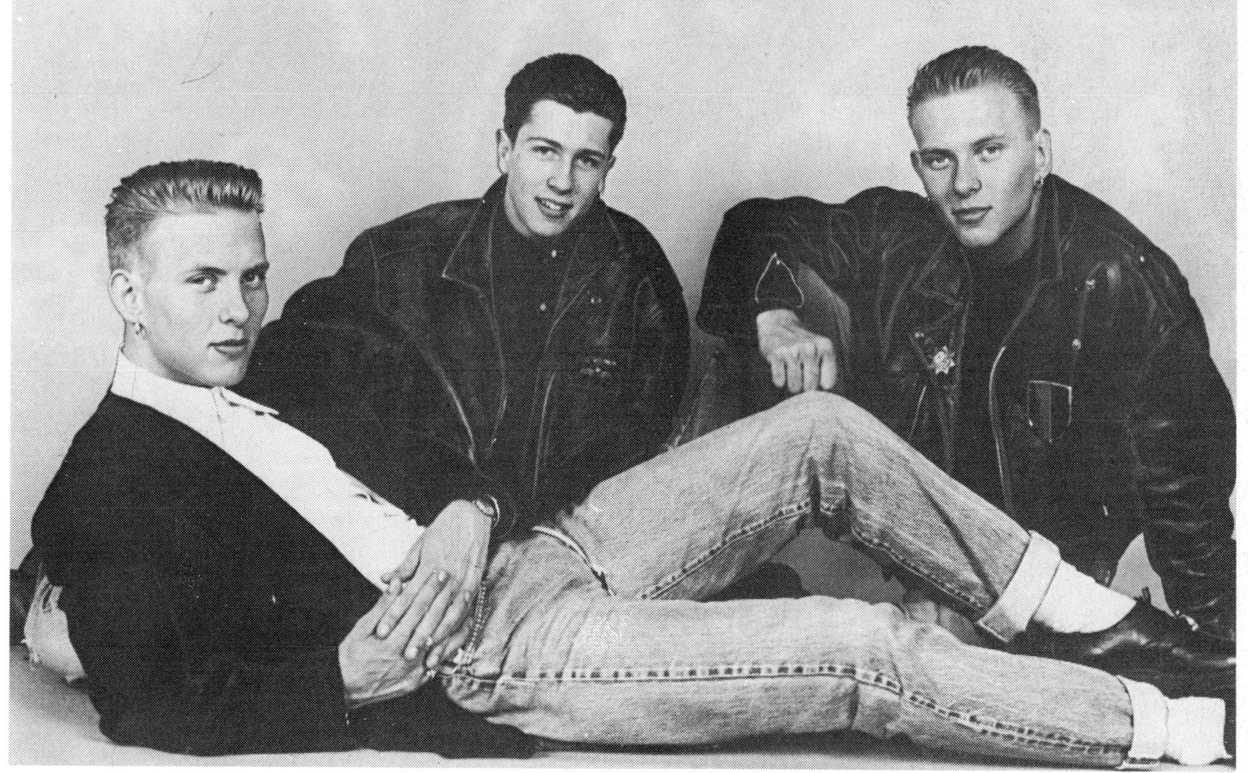

JILL'S PHOTO FILE

Dear Jill,

All my friends get to wear make-up and trendy clothes, and are allowed to style their hair in different ways. My parents are really old-fashioned, and my mum still chooses my clothes for me! It's really making me miserable . . .

SEE YOU LATER. WE'RE OFF TO THE YOUTH CLUB DISCO . . .
YOU LOOK VERY NICE, DEAR. YOUR DAD WILL PICK YOU AND ELLEN UP AT TEN.

Jill says . . .

Mums and Dads never give in to things like wearing make-up easily, and it's best not to go behind their backs. The thing to do is to behave in a mature way, and to let them know gradually that you're ready to wear make-up, choose your own clothes, etc. Let them see that you can behave responsibly when you DO get the chance to choose something new or to try out make-up. Whatever you do, don't go over the top with outrageously trendy clothes or make-up! That'll only convince your mum and dad that you're NOT ready to choose for yourself.

Then —
HOW ABOUT THIS DRESS, LINDA? IT'S JUST THE THING FOR YOUR COUSIN'S WEDDING.
YUK!
WELL, I'LL TRY IT ON, MUM — BUT COULD I PICK OUT SOMETHING MYSELF TO TRY ON AS WELL?

I'M GLAD YOUR DAD'S PICKING US UP, LINDA. MY DAD WOULD NEVER BOTHER.
YEAH — MUM AND DAD ARE GOOD IN SOME WAYS, BUT THEY'RE SO OLD-FASHIONED. I'M FED UP LOOKING SO SQUARE.

TELL YOU WHAT — I'LL PUT SOME MAKE-UP ON YOU WHEN WE GET TO THE DISCO.
HUH — I'D JUST HAVE TO TAKE IT OFF AGAIN BEFORE DAD SAW ME. HE'D GO SPARE!

Later —
HAVE A GOOD TIME, LINDA?
YEAH, IT WAS OKAY, I SUPPOSE. DIDN'T ELLEN LOOK GREAT TONIGHT? SHE'S REALLY TRENDY.

MMM, WELL — I THOUGHT SHE LOOKED AWFUL. SHE WAS WEARING FAR TOO MUCH MAKE-UP.
AND YOUNG GIRLS DON'T NEED TO DRESS THEMSELVES UP LIKE THAT — YOU CERTAINLY DON'T, LINDA. YOU'RE PRETTY ENOUGH AS YOU ARE.

THIS IS WHAT I'D REALLY LIKE, MUM. IF YOU BOUGHT ME THIS I'D BE ABLE TO WEAR IT TO DISCOS, TOO.
WELL, IT'S NOT WHAT I'D CHOOSE FOR YOU, BUT IT DOESN'T LOOK TOO BAD, I SUPPOSE. ALL RIGHT, LINDA.

The day of the wedding —
HEY, MUM — THIS PALE LIPSTICK'S ACE. COULD I PUT ON A LITTLE FOR THE WEDDING?
WELL, I SUPPOSE A LITTLE WON'T HURT.

I'VE LET LINDA PUT A LITTLE LIPSTICK ON — AND I THINK IT REALLY SUITS HER.
WHAT A PAIR OF SMASHERS. YOU BOTH LOOK GREAT.

WELL, IT'S A START. I'LL LET THEM SEE THAT I'M NOT GOING TO GO MAD WITH MAKE-UP AND MY CLOTHES. THINGS ARE LOOKING UP!

The Hi! Soap The Valley Girls

BEV, Zoe, Kay and Linda all lived on the Valley estate. One day, Bev was engrossed in her magazine . . .

HMM, THIS ARTICLE IN MY MAGAZINE SAYS IT'S OKAY TO ASK A BOY OUT . . . HUH — FAT CHANCE. I'D NEVER HAVE THE NERVE . . .
The phone rang —
HELLO — 228 23670 . . .
OH . . . I THINK I'VE GOT THE WRONG NUMBER. THAT'S NOT OUR PRICE RECORD SHOP, IS IT? I WANT TO KNOW IF THEY'VE GOT THE WETS LATEST ALBUM IN YET.
ER, NO — NOT QUITE! IN FACT, THERE ISN'T EVEN AN "OUR PRICE" IN OUR TOWN. YOU REALLY HAVE GOT THE WRONG NUMBER!
IT'S A BOY . . . HE SOUNDS ABOUT MY AGE. HE'S GOT A REALLY NICE VOICE . . .
CRIKEY! OH, WELL — WHO CARES ABOUT THE WETS ANYWAY? YOU SOUND MUCH NICER . . . MY NAME'S GARY. WHAT'S YOURS?
ER . . . BEV!
WOW! I'M GETTING CHATTED UP. I DON'T BELIEVE IT!
TEA, BEV!
WHO WAS THAT ON THE PHONE, LOVE?
OH, IT WAS JUST A WRONG NUMBER, MUM.
GARY SAID HE MIGHT RING AGAIN. OH, I HOPE HE DOES!
Meanwhile, at Kay's house —
STOP THIS ONE, LINDA!
HEY! WHAT DO YOU THINK I AM, ZOE — A GIRAFFE?

OH! OH! THE BALL'S GONE INTO GRANNY PORTER'S GARDEN!
SHE'LL LET US HAVE IT BACK, WON'T SHE, KAY?
KNOWING HER, I WOULDN'T BANK ON IT!

ALL RIGHT, BUT JUST THIS ONCE. CAN'T I GET ANY PEACE? NEXT TIME A BALL COMES OVER HERE I'LL KEEP IT! GOT IT?
I PITY KAY, LIVING NEXT DOOR TO AN OLD RATBAG LIKE HER!

Next morning, there was only one thing on Bev's mind —
I WONDER IF GARY **WILL** PHONE AGAIN? HE SOUNDED REALLY DREAMY. BUT I DON'T SUPPOSE HE WILL . . . NOTHING EXCITING EVER HAPPENS TO ME!

But a few hours later —
HELLO? YES — THIS IS BEV!
IT'S HIM! YIPPEE!
HOI! GET OUT OF THE WAY, BEV! D'YOU HAVE TO SPRAWL ALL OVER THE STAIRS LIKE THAT? HONESTLY — LITTLE SISTERS!

A long while later —
THAT WAS ACE! WE'VE GOT LOTS AND LOTS IN COMMON. GARY'S GIVEN ME HIS NUMBER SO I CAN RING HIM AS WELL. HE LIVES QUITE FAR AWAY, THOUGH — SO I'D BETTER NOT TELL MUM AND DAD. THEY'D ONLY MOAN ABOUT THE PHONE BILL.
Back at Kay's —
THAT'S FUNNY . . . I CAN SMELL BURNING. BUT I KNOW I HAVEN'T LEFT ANYTHING ON THE COOKER . . .

OH! IT'S COMING FROM GRANNY PORTER'S HOUSE! DAD! DAD — RING THE FIRE BRIGADE!

GRANNY PORTER — ARE YOU IN THERE?
SHE'S AT BINGO, LOVE. WHAT'S WRONG?
THERE'S A FIRE! MY DAD'S PHONED THE FIRE BRIGADE!

OH, THANK GOODNESS — HERE THEY ARE!
ALL RIGHT, LOVE — MOVE AWAY FROM THERE. ANYONE IN THE BUILDING? WE'LL SEE TO THIS . . .

Minutes later —
HERE! WHAT'S GOING ON? THAT'S MY HOUSE!
YOU LEFT THE IRON PLUGGED IN. FIRE'S OUT NOW. LUCKY THE LASS SPOTTED THE SMOKE WHEN SHE DID, OR THERE COULD HAVE BEEN A WHOLE LOT MORE DAMAGE.

THANKS, KAY. I KNOW I MOAN A LOT AT YOU YOUNGSTERS, BUT I'M REALLY GRATEFUL.
THAT'S OKAY, GRANNY. I COULD HARDLY LET YOUR HOUSE BURN DOWN, COULD I?

Bev couldn't wait to phone Gary —
IT'S SAFE TO RING GARY NOW — MUM AND DAD ARE BOTH BUSY. OH, I CAN'T WAIT TO HEAR HIS VOICE!

But two minutes later —
I MANAGED TO GET THE WETS ALBUM, BEV — IT'S ACE . . .
OH — MUM!
ER — RIGHT, KAY. GLAD THAT'S SORTED OUT, THEN — SEE YOU IN SCHOOL TOMORROW. 'BYE!

THAT WAS KAY, MUM. SHE RANG ME FOR HELP WITH OUR HOMEWORK!
THAT'S FUNNY, LOVE — I DIDN'T HEAR THE PHONE RINGING. OH, WELL . . .

. . . SO THAT'S WHY I CALLED YOU KAY! SORRY. DID YOU THINK I'D GONE DAFT? ONLY MY PARENTS WOULD GO SPARE IF THEY KNEW I WAS PHONING LONG DISTANCE.
YEAH, MINE TOO. STILL IT'S WORTH IT. I REALLY ENJOY OUR LITTLE CHATS, BEV.

OOH — GARY'S GREAT. HE SAYS REALLY NICE THINGS. THIS IS THE BEST THING THAT'S HAPPENED TO ME IN AGES!

Kay was dyeing Linda's hair —
YOUR HAIR'LL LOOK GREAT WITH THESE RED HIGHLIGHTS, LINDA.
I HOPE SO, KAY. IT SAYS TO LEAVE IT FOR HALF AN HOUR . . .

But twenty minutes later —

CRIKEY, KAY — THE STREAKS'VE GONE GREEN! WHAT A SIGHT!

QUICK — WE'LL TRY AND WASH IT OUT BEFORE YOUR MUM SEES IT!

But then —

LINDA! OH, MY GOODNESS — WHAT HAVE YOU DONE?

MRS CARTWRIGHT!

ER — I WAS JUST HIGHLIGHTING MY HAIR, MUM. WE COULDN'T HELP IT GOING WRONG . . .
DEAR, OH, DEAR! I'LL PHONE THE HAIRDRESSER'S. I JUST HOPE THEY CAN FIT YOU IN AT SHORT NOTICE. LET THIS BE A LESSON TO YOU NOT TO MESS ABOUT WITH YOUR HAIR AGAIN!
YOU'RE IN LUCK — WE'VE HAD A CANCELLATION. DON'T WORRY — WE'LL MAKE YOU PRESENTABLE AGAIN.
THANK GOODNESS. I DON'T WANT ANYONE TO SEE ME LIKE THIS, OR I'D NEVER LIVE IT DOWN! MUM'S BERET'S DOING A GREAT JOB COVERING UP MY GREEN STREAKS!
But —
WHY, HELLO, LINDA . . .
OH, NO — IT'S GRANNY PORTER, THE WORST GOSSIP IN THE WHOLE OF THE VALLEY. SHE'LL TELL EVERYONE! OH . . . JUST MY LUCK!
On Thursday evening, Gary rang Bev —
BEV! GREAT NEWS — I'VE SAVED UP THE TRAIN FARE, AND I'M COMING TO SEE YOU ON SATURDAY! WE CAN MEET, FACE TO FACE! THAT'LL BE MORE FUN THAN JUST TALKING ON THE PHONE, WON'T IT?
WH-WHAT? OH — ER — YES! ER — THAT'S WONDERFUL, GARY! ER — I CAN'T TALK NOW. MUM'S CALLING ME . . . SEE YOU ON SATURDAY!
Bev fled to her room —
OH, NO! I TOLD HIM I WAS SLIM AND PRETTY — I NEVER THOUGHT WE'D ACTUALLY MEET. WHEN HE DOES SEE ME, ALL FAT AND GLASSES — HE'LL NEVER WANT TO TALK TO ME AGAIN! OH, CRIKEY — I FEEL SICK!
All too soon it was Saturday —
THIS IS IT. I'VE PUT ON MY BEST GEAR, BUT I — I BET HE'LL TAKE ONE LOOK AND GO AWAY AGAIN.
BEV! THERE'S A FRIEND OF YOURS COME TO CALL FOR YOU — GARY PRESTON.

HI, BEV. IT'S GREAT TO MEET YOU AT LAST!
OH! HE — HE'S SORT OF CHUBBY, TOO. BUT — HE'S GOT LOVELY EYES, AND A NICE SMILE . . .
Gary took Bev for a burger —
I'M STARVING! LET'S HAVE A DOUBLE PORTION OF CHIPS. YOU'RE NOT ON A DIET OR ANYTHING DAFT, ARE YOU?
WELL . . . SORT OF . . .
WELL, DON'T BE. YOU'RE NICE JUST AS YOU ARE, BEV. NOT ALL BOYS LIKE SKINNY GIRLS, YOU KNOW!
OH, GARY'S THE NICEST BOY I'VE EVER MET!
Gary and Bev spent a happy day together —
MY MUM AND DAD ARE NAGGING ABOUT THE PHONE BILLS, BEV — SO I WON'T BE ABLE TO RING SO OFTEN. BUT I WAS THINKING — WE COULD WRITE TO EACH OTHER, COULDN'T WE?
OH, YES! THAT'D BE GREAT! I LOVE GETTING LETTERS . . .
. . . ESPECIALLY FROM A SMASHING BOY LIKE YOU!
AND I MIGHT BE ABLE TO COME AND SEE YOU AGAIN QUITE SOON. I'LL SAVE UP REALLY HARD. BYE, BEV.
OOH!
HE KISSED ME! AND HE WANTS TO KEEP IN TOUCH . . . AND HE SAID HE'LL COME AGAIN! I'VE STILL GOT MY SPECIAL BOYFRIEND. OH, THIS IS THE BEST DAY OF MY WHOLE LIFE!
the end

A READER'S TRUE STORY

I WANTED A BOYFRIEND

WHEN my best friend, Rosie, found a boyfriend, that was the last straw! Nearly all the girls in our class were going out with boys — and now Rosie too! Why not me?

All they ever seemed to chat about was their dates — where they'd been, what they'd said to each other — I was always left out. That's what made me determined — I had to find a boyfriend too. I wasn't going to be the odd one out any more.

There were two boys at school that I really fancied — Scott Donovan and Ian Mason, but they never really seemed interested in me. I was beginning to think I'd never get a date at all — when suddenly Brian Foote asked me out.

Brian didn't go to our school, but I knew him from the Youth Club. To be honest, I'd never really liked him that much. On club nights, he used to just hang around with his mates — never really joining in — just making fun of other people and cracking unkind jokes.

Usually I kept well clear of them. But when I met Brian at a bus stop one day and he asked me out, I immediately pushed all his bad points out of my mind. At least he was a boy. And he'd asked me out!

I felt really great going into school the next day and saying I'd got a date too. At lunchtime when everyone was discussing what they'd wear the next time they went out with their boyfriends, I could join in. It felt good.

But compared to the fun I'd had at school, the date itself was a bit of a let down.

We'd arranged to go to the cinema and to start with, Brian was ten minutes late. I went through agonies as I waited for him. I was scared I'd have to go to school the next day and admit I'd been stood up.

It was such a relief when he actually turned up, but my pleasure soon turned to disappointment again when we reached the cinema ticket office and Brian told me bluntly that I'd have to pay for myself. Luckily I'd brought enough money!

Once inside, things got rapidly worse. It was a good film and I wanted to watch it — but Brian had other things on his mind. He kept nibbling my ear, and trying to kiss me. I didn't fancy him at all, and besides, there were people sitting right next to us. I really wished he'd pack it in.

All in all, I didn't enjoy our date very much. But when he asked me out again, I eagerly said yes. No matter how horrid Brian was, at least now I had a boyfriend!

Back at school, things were really great. It was lovely to be able to join in all the chat about boyfriends. Now I felt one of the crowd whereas before I'd often wondered if some of the girls were secretly sniggering at me because I was the only one without a boyfriend.

If only my dates with Brian could have been as much fun. But they weren't. He was always late, and seemed to spend all his time trying to manoeuvre me into a dark corner somewhere so he could start slobbering all over me. I hated it!

But worse than that, was the way he often behaved to other people. We were walking through the park one day and Brian deliberately dropped his drink can on the grass — even though there was a litter bin really close by. An old man shouted at him to pick it up and Brian was really nasty. He yelled rude names at the man and threatened he'd get him one day. I felt really embarrassed.

That wasn't the only time he was rude to other people either. One night there were two old ladies standing at the bus stop with us, and he insulted them.

I felt really ashamed being with him. But then I told myself that I was being silly.

After all, at least he was a boyfriend, even if he wasn't my ideal one. I could put up with him — I had to. It was better than not having a boyfriend at all.

But then came the day when I changed my mind.

Brian and I were walking down the road and two women were walking towards us. They were holding bags full of shopping and they were taking up most of the pavement — but it didn't bother me. I just automatically squeezed up against the wall to let them pass — but not Brian.

He swaggered straight towards them, told them rudely that they took up so much room because they were fat, and then barged straight between the two of them, knocking them flying. Their shopping went all over the place.

"Come on! Let's get out of here!" he said. But I couldn't just run away.

The poor women were desperately trying to catch tins before they rolled away, and rescue things from the mess a box of broken eggs and a smashed bottle of squash had made. I couldn't just run off and leave them to it.

So I shook my head at Brian, and walked back to help the women as best I could.

Out of the corner of my eye, I could see him run off, and I knew he'd never speak to me again because I hadn't gone with him. But suddenly I didn't care any more.

"What a dreadful boy!" one of the women muttered, as she cleared up. And I knew she was right.

Brian *was* dreadful. He was rude and selfish. He couldn't behave properly, and he didn't care about anyone else's feelings — including mine. That wasn't the kind of person I wanted as my boyfriend.

Of course I knew I'd have to go back to school tomorrow and admit I was boyfriendless again. But so what? I might not have a boyfriend, but at least I had my pride. It wasn't much fun being on my own when all my mates had steadies — but then it wasn't much fun going out with a yob like Brian either.

So, in future, I decided, I'd stay on my own — until someone I *really* liked asked me out.

Hi! BROTHER BEYOND

A GIRL LIKE THAT

MIND YOUR OWN BUSINESS.

TRYING TO SNEAK OFF EARLY ARE YOU, LORNA?

LORNA had just started at Donna's school.

THAT NEW GIRL'S REALLY THICK, ISN'T SHE?

YEAH. I HEAR SHE HAS A POLICE RECORD TOO.

COME OFF IT, DONNA! I'VE HEARD HER DAD'S IN PRISON.

THAT'S A BIT UNFAIR. YOU DON'T KNOW IF THAT'S REALLY TRUE.

EVERYONE'S BEING REALLY HORRIBLE TO LORNA BEFORE SHE'S HAD A CHANCE TO PROVE HERSELF. IF HER DAD **IS** IN PRISON IT CAN'T BE MUCH FUN FOR HER OR HER MUM.

WHEN I SPOKE TO HER SHE SEEMED OKAY. WELL, I'M NOT GOING TO BE HORRIBLE TO HER — I'M GOING TO TRY TO BE FRIENDLY.

Donna's chance came the next day —
THIS PROJECT IS ABOUT THE ENVIRONMENT. I WANT TO SEE HOW MUCH TRAFFIC PASSES THE SCHOOL AT DIFFERENT TIMES IN THE SCHOOL DAY. YOU CAN EITHER DO IT IN PAIRS OR ON YOUR OWN.

So Donna asked Lorna to help her —
YOU WANT TO DO YOUR PROJECT WITH ME?
YEAH. WHY NOT? I'D RATHER WORK IN A PAIR. IT'LL BE MORE FUN.

But when Donna's mates found out —
YOU MUST BE DAFT, ASKING HER TO HELP YOU. SHE'LL PROBABLY USE IT AS AN EXCUSE TO BUNK OFF SCHOOL FOR THE MORNING.
NO SHE WON'T. I KNOW WHAT I'M DOING.

Next day —
WE SHOULD MONITOR THE TRAFFIC MORNING, LUNCH-TIME AND AFTERNOONS. THAT WAY WE'LL SEE HOW IT AFFECTS US WHEN WE'RE GOING IN OR OUT OF SCHOOL.
YEAH! AND WE CAN DIVIDE THE TRAFFIC INTO GROUPS LIKE LORRIES AND CARS.

THAT'S A GOOD IDEA. THE BIGGER THE VEHICLE THE MORE FUMES THERE MUST BE AND THE MORE WEAR AND TEAR ON THE ROAD.
LORNA'S REALLY INTO THIS. I'M PLEASED I ASKED HER.

HEY, DONNA! THAT BLOKE IN THAT CAR WAVED TO US.
LORNA SEEMS TO BE RELAXING A BIT. SHE MUST BE ENJOYING THIS.

Later —

WHAT ARE YOU HAVING FOR TEA TONIGHT, LORNA?

PROBABLY NOTHING. MUM'S GOT TO PICK MY LITTLE BROTHER UP AND SHE'S ALWAYS TOO TIRED AFTER WORK.

WELL MY MUM AND DAD WON'T BE IN TILL AFTER SIX. WHY DON'T YOU COME AND HAVE SOME TEA AT MY PLACE? I'LL DO BEANS ON TOAST.

OKAY. THANKS, DONNA.

THIS HOUSE IS NICE. WHAT DO YOUR MUM AND DAD DO?

OH, THEY'VE GOT A BUSINESS. WHAT ABOUT YOURS?

MY DAD'S IN PRISON SO MUM HAS TO WORK. SHE GETS REALLY DEPRESSED THOUGH, SO I HAVE TO LOOK AFTER MY BROTHER A LOT.

I'M SORRY. THAT CAN'T BE MUCH FUN.

IT MUST BE GREAT HAVING A MUM AND DAD WITH LOTS OF MONEY.
I DON'T KNOW. THEY'RE SO BUSY MAKING THE MONEY I DON'T GET TO SEE THAT MUCH OF THEM.

ANYWAY, I'LL GO AND MAKE US SOMETHING TO EAT.
ALL RIGHT. I'LL HAVE A LOOK AT SOME OF YOUR OLD "Hi!s".

LORNA REALLY SEEMS TO LIKE ME. I KNEW SHE WAS OKAY, BUT NOBODY ELSE BELIEVED ME.

But at the weekend —
COME ON, DONNA! WE'LL BE LATE FOR LUNCH AT AUNTIE JO'S.
COMING, MUM. I'M JUST LOOKING FOR GRAN'S PENDANT.

THAT'S FUNNY. IT'S GONE. IT WAS HERE WHEN I SHOWED IT TO LORNA ON WEDNESDAY.

OH, NO! LORNA MUST HAVE TAKEN IT WHEN I WAS IN THE KITCHEN. WHAT AM I GOING TO DO?

WHAT CAN I TELL MUM? I CAN'T TELL HER LORNA TOOK IT.
DONNA! WILL YOU HURRY UP!

WHAT'S THE MATTER? WHERE'S YOUR PENDANT?
IT — IT'S NOT HERE.

WHERE IS IT THEN? WHEN DID YOU LAST HAVE IT?
WHEN I SHOWED IT TO LORNA ON WEDNESDAY.

WELL, THAT SPEAKS FOR ITSELF, DOESN'T IT? LORNA'S TAKEN IT. I KNEW I SHOULDN'T HAVE LET YOU BRING A GIRL LIKE THAT INTO THE HOUSE.
YOU DON'T KNOW LORNA HAS TAKEN IT, MUM. I MEAN, JUST BECAUSE HER DAD IS IN PRISON DOESN'T MEAN **SHE'S** A THIEF!

OH NO? YOU GAVE HER A CHANCE AND LOOK HOW SHE PAYS YOU BACK. DONNA! WHERE ARE YOU GOING?
TO SEE LORNA AND CLEAR HER NAME.

SURELY LORNA WOULDN'T HAVE TAKEN MY PENDANT? AFTER ALL, I'VE BEEN SO NICE TO HER. SHE OWES ME SOMETHING BETTER THAN THIS.

ER, HI, LORNA! I'D LIKE A WORD WITH YOU ON YOUR OWN.
OH, HI, DONNA! I DIDN'T EXPECT TO SEE YOU HERE TODAY.

GO AND GET YOURSELF A DRINK, PAUL. DONNA WANTS TO SPEAK TO ME.
OH, ALL RIGHT.

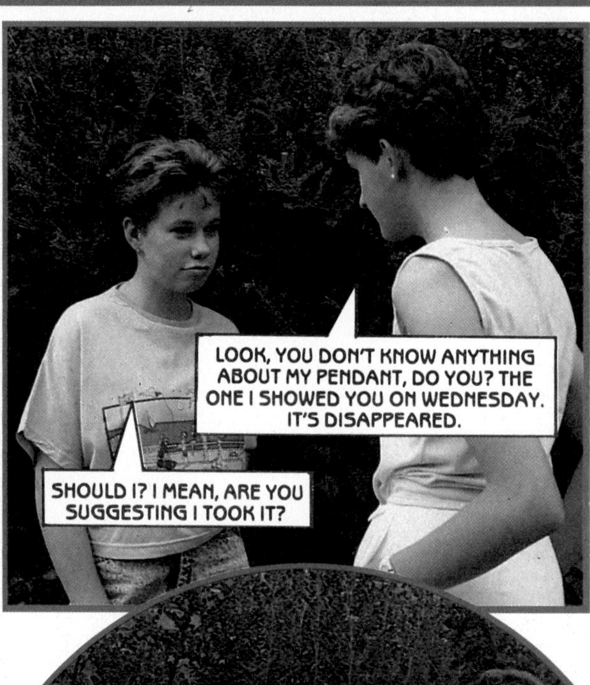
LOOK, YOU DON'T KNOW ANYTHING ABOUT MY PENDANT, DO YOU? THE ONE I SHOWED YOU ON WEDNESDAY. IT'S DISAPPEARED.
SHOULD I? I MEAN, ARE YOU SUGGESTING I TOOK IT?

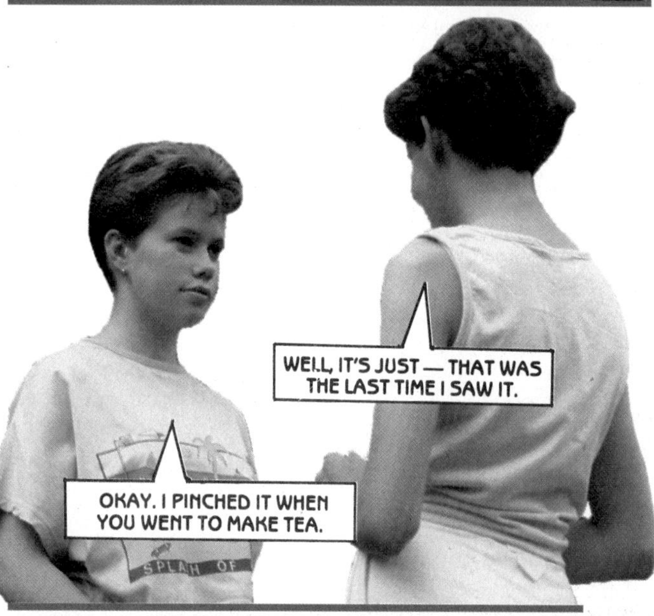
WELL, IT'S JUST — THAT WAS THE LAST TIME I SAW IT.
OKAY. I PINCHED IT WHEN YOU WENT TO MAKE TEA.

HOW COULD YOU? WHY BE SO ROTTEN AFTER ALL I'VE DONE FOR YOU?
'COS I **AM** ROTTEN, THAT'S WHY. ANYONE I'VE EVER THOUGHT ANYTHING OF HAS HURT ME, SO I THOUGHT I'D HURT YOU FIRST.
BUT I DON'T WANT TO HURT YOU, LORNA!
I'M NOT DAFT, DONNA. YOU'LL GET TIRED OF ME. I KNOW YOU ONLY ASKED ME TO HELP WITH THE PROJECT BECAUSE YOU FELT SORRY FOR ME.

I'M A SORT OF PROJECT TOO, AREN'T I? SOMETHING TO AMUSE YOU AS YOUR PARENTS DON'T HAVE TIME FOR YOU.
THAT'S NOT TRUE!

HOW DARE YOU SAY THAT ABOUT MY PARENTS? THEY'VE BEEN REALLY KIND TO YOU!
OH, GIVE IT A REST! HERE'S YOUR PENDANT. I DON'T WANT IT.

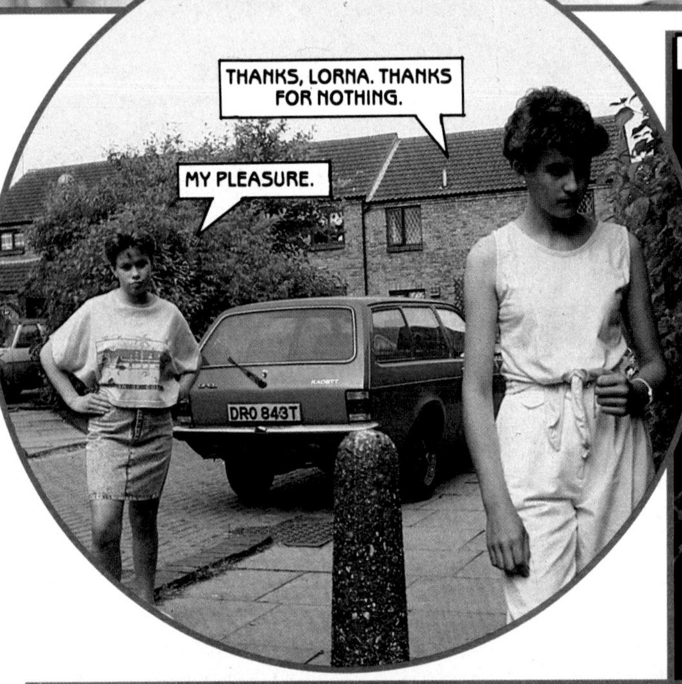
THANKS, LORNA. THANKS FOR NOTHING.
MY PLEASURE.
DRO 843T

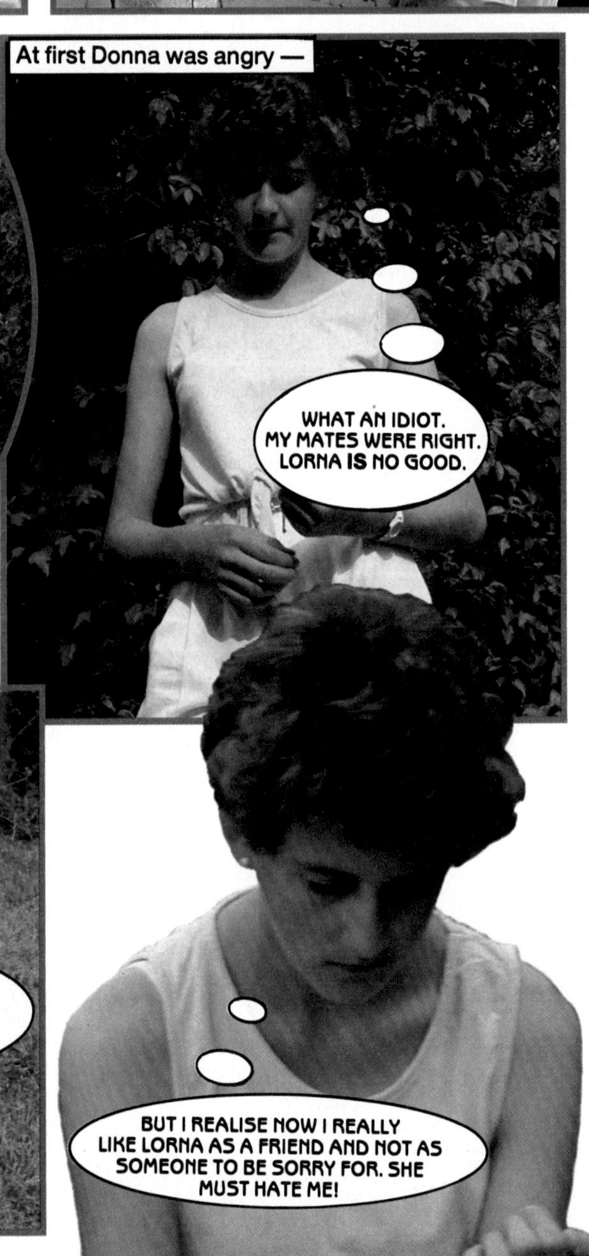
At first Donna was angry —
WHAT AN IDIOT. MY MATES WERE RIGHT. LORNA IS NO GOOD.
BUT I REALISE NOW I REALLY LIKE LORNA AS A FRIEND AND NOT AS SOMEONE TO BE SORRY FOR. SHE MUST HATE ME!

But then —
MAYBE LORNA'S RIGHT. I DID FEEL SORRY FOR HER AND IT WAS LIKE HAVING A PROJECT. BEING NICE TO HER MADE ME FEEL GOOD.

I MUST GO AND APOLOGISE . . . OR AT LEAST EXPLAIN. I HOPE SHE DOESN'T SLAM THE DOOR IN MY FACE.

OH, IT'S YOU AGAIN. WHAT DO YOU WANT — BROUGHT THE POLICE, HAVE YOU?
NO. I'VE COME TO APOLOGISE.

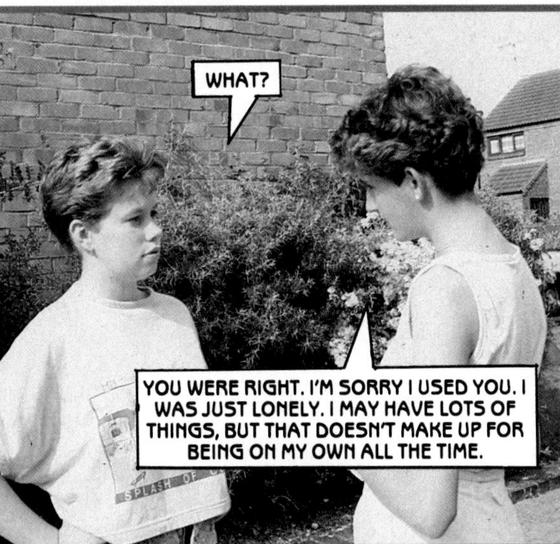
WHAT?
YOU WERE RIGHT. I'M SORRY I USED YOU. I WAS JUST LONELY. I MAY HAVE LOTS OF THINGS, BUT THAT DOESN'T MAKE UP FOR BEING ON MY OWN ALL THE TIME.

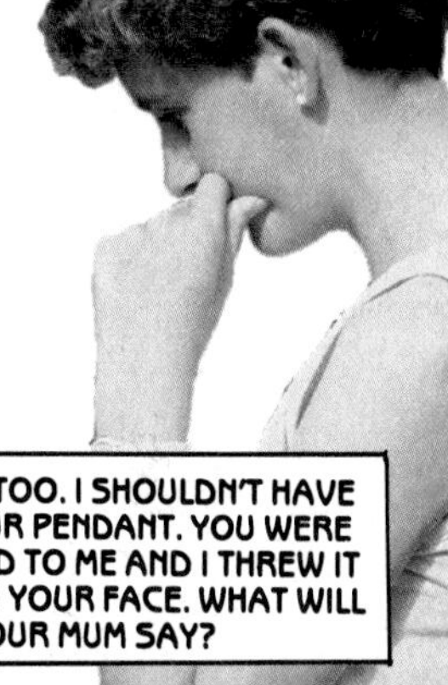
I DID TRY TO BE FRIENDS FOR ALL THE WRONG REASONS, BUT I REALISE NOW I WANT TO BE PROPER MATES, IF THAT'S OKAY.
I'M SORRY TOO. I SHOULDN'T HAVE TAKEN YOUR PENDANT. YOU WERE REALLY KIND TO ME AND I THREW IT ALL BACK IN YOUR FACE. WHAT WILL YOUR MUM SAY?

SHE'LL COME ROUND I GUESS. I COULD SAY YOU BORROWED IT.
NO, TELL HER THE TRUTH. MAYBE SHE'LL SEE SHE SHOULD SPEND MORE TIME WITH YOU. AREN'T YOU SUPPOSED TO BE AT YOUR AUNTIE'S WITH HER?

OH, I FORGOT . . .
OH, WELL, COME AND HAVE SOME TEA WITH ME AND PAUL INSTEAD. IT'S ONLY BEANS ON TOAST, BUT . . .
SOUNDS GREAT TO ME!
the end

GET IT

There's no point in having a wardrobe full of clothes if you don't know how to wear them. Just flinging on any old thing that's clean rarely looks good, so here we show you what to do (and what NOT to do!).

WRONG
Jeans are meant to be casual and comfy, so don't wear your six-inch stilettos with them. Shoes like these are neither comfy nor casual and are too dressy for jeans. The blouse our model is wearing is also dressy with a wide neck and the weight of the denim jacket is pulling it out of line.

RIGHT
This looks much better — jeans with flat, comfy loafers and a stretch cotton top. You'll be able to walk miles in these shoes without getting sore feet or breaking your ankle when you fall off them! Also, because the top is a wrap-round style it fits snugly and the jacket doesn't pull it down.

RIGHT!

WRONG
This looks completely ridiculous and isn't flattering to the figure at all. Because the top has been tightly belted over a gathered skirt it's lumpy and doesn't sit properly making our model look as though she has big hips. Also, with the different wedges of colour, it looks as though the body is in sections and this creates an illusion of shortness. Wearing ankle socks with shoes like these makes the legs look short and stumpy.

RIGHT
With the shirt tucked in you can see the difference. The model looks much slimmer, as you can see her waist instead of lumps and folds of fabric. The solid block of black on her bottom half makes her look much slimmer. The ankle boots are much better with this outfit, as the shirt is casual and the stripy tights liven everything up.

GET IT RIGHT!

WRONG

These trousers can be casual or dressy, but this t-shirt doesn't match at all. It looks as though you can't make up your mind whether you want to dress up (shoes with heels) or slop around (bright t-shirt). Apart from everything else none of the colours match and it almost looks like an explosion in a paint factory!

RIGHT

What a difference! The outfit now looks smart and co-ordinated. The colours tone in and the red roses on the waistcoat add a touch of brightness. The outfit could be casual, but is instantly smartened up when the waistcoat is added.

Follow these guidelines and get the most from your clothes.

- Try to buy colours that tone in with each other so that you can mix and match more. This increases the size of your wardrobe.
- Black is always a good basic colour and you can add different coloured accessories to brighten it up.
- Beige, cream, navy and white are also colours which tone well with brighter colours or each other.
- You can easily change the look of an outfit by adding different accessories — you DON'T need to buy a whole new outfit.
- Plain, dark colours are more slimming and flattering to the figure than bright, fussy prints. So, if you want to disguise a big bum, don't draw attention to it by wearing your fluorescent beach shorts!
- Don't spend a fortune on an outrageous item of clothing if you know you'll only wear it once. This is especially true at Sale time — a bargain's only a bargain if you know you'll get a lot of wear out of it. Good buys from sales are classic items such as jeans, loafers or a simple black blazer.
- Finally, don't worry if you do have some fashion disasters in your wardrobe, EVERYBODY does. Here's some of ours —

Liz: Burgundy, cord knickerbockers with lace-up sides that were all the rage when the New Romantic look was in *yonks* ago. I used to wear them with a hideous frilly shirt and I must have looked really stupid.

Jill: A horrid pair of bright pink dungarees that make me look like a pregnant clown. I keep them to wear when I'm decorating my flat or something, but I never do because they make me look so ridiculous.

Chief Sub: A really awful shawl that I knitted myself and I was dead pleased with it at the time. It's like something a hippy would wear and I think it'll be going to line the cats' basket soon!

Pop Ed: An extremely loud red and black checked coat dress that makes me look like a walking tablecloth.

Fiction Ed: A black and silver lurex dress — need I say more!

Features Ed: A crimplene strapless sundress that cost £3 in a sale. I bought it for a summer holiday and it was so horrible I left it in the hotel!

The Ed: A white, lacy cardi that my auntie gave me for a birthday present. I hate it but I can't throw it out just in case she asks about it!

PICK OF THE PACK

Every one is someone's favourite! There's a Brat out there for YOU and we're going to help you find him!

RIVER PHOENIX— THE ROMANTIC

River Jade Phoenix is the brat for you if you're into flowers and chocolates. He's the caring type of guy who'd make sure you had every little thing your beating heart desired.

A real home-loving guy, your first date together might be dinner at his house. He'd want you to meet his brother and sisters — Leaf, Rainbow, Summer and Liberty! (Bit embarrassing if your name's plain old Jane!)

River would rustle up something nice and healthy for dinner — this boy looks after himself, you know — and afterwards you'd sit together on the porch as the sun sets. River would strum a few tunes on his old 'geetar' and you'd talk about the stars. Aaah — so romantic!

Folks say he's a bit of a dreamer, but after the first date you can bet that YOU would be the only one in his dreams.

ROB LOWE — THE SMOOTHIE

If it's class you're after then Rob's the guy for you. A date with him would definitely call for some serious dressing up. He's a big fan of designer suits — so maybe your best ripped jeans just WOULDN'T do!

Of course, if you didn't fancy an evening bopping at the disco, Rob may take you for a picnic in the country. He likes nothing better than driving out in the peace and quiet and spending the day with his dog, Wolfie. He drives a pretty snazzy car — a Mustang — so we bet he's not the slowest driver on Earth!

You wouldn't be expected to provide the sandwiches, either. Rob, being a bit of a toff, would have the best restaurant in Beverly Hills make those. And HE'D make the dessert — his famous chocolate mousse!

Imagine walking in the country, the wind blowing through your hair and Rob by your side — WOW!

TOM CRUISE — THE HUNK

Tom's got the smile that puts the other Brats to shame! He also believes in looking after himself — which makes him a bit of an action man. You'd have to be super-fit to keep up with our Tom!

He didn't mind the rigorous work-outs which were needed to prepare him for his part in 'Top Gun' and as we all saw in 'Cocktail' he's continued to 'work that body'.

If you don't like speed then Tom's not the guy for you. There's nothing he likes better than racing about on his Ninja motorcycle — or speeding round the track in a racing car.

We reckon the chase would be worth it if you could catch Tom 'cos there certainly wouldn't be a dull moment with him around.

If Tom's the guy for you, then hold on to your hat!

ANDREW McCARTHY — THE BOY NEXT DOOR

Andrew's the type of guy your mother would love you to date! You won't find his name linked with any scandal — and you definitely wouldn't find him wearing anything as untidy as ripped jeans!

The gentleman of the pack, his favourite pastime is going to the cinema or even posher — to the theatre. Expect a fab nosh-up at a good restaurant if you're on a date with Andy-baby, 'cos he likes his grub.

Underneath that gentlemanly exterior there lies a bit of an imp, so don't worry about being bored, 'cos Andrew won't be quiet for long. He'll whisk you round the New York sights so fast that you won't know what's hit you!

KEIFER SUTHERLAND — THE TOUGH GUY

Keifer William Frederick Dempsey George Rufus Sutherland (phew!) is someone who won't be messed around with! Remember him in 'The Lost Boys'? No one's going to kick sand in HIS face!

You'd have to have quite an outgoing personality to hang about with Keifer 'cos he likes everyone to know he's around. Don't be put off by the evil parts he plays — he's not all bad. Underneath that tough exterior he's really a big softie.

He's not exactly a snazzy dresser so turning up in your old jeans and leather jacket will probably go down a treat. Anyway, you'd look daft eating a Big Mac in a posh frock — no fancy food for Keifer!

If you like a bit of action you'll have a brill time with Keifer. As the boy himself would say, "Be there or be square!".

NOT FOUND THE BRAT FOR YOU YET? HERE ARE SOME MORE FOR YOU TO DROOL OVER.

PATRICK DEMPSEY

This boy would certainly keep you amused — he's a juggler, unicyclist and a ventriloquist! Never a dull moment with Paddy around! Don't be surprised if a date with Patrick ends up with HIM being the main attraction — he's a born performer.

MATTHEW BRODERICK

The twinkle in his eye reveals the fun-side of his nature. Although he shuns the limelight that doesn't mean he's a stick-in-the-mud. Matthew's a guaranteed funster!

JOHNNY DEPP

This boy's a serious 'rawk 'n' roller' — so be prepared to dance! He's a major-mover so put your best dancing shoes on and get ready to boogie-on- down!

Alone!

PART 3

continued from page 53

CHEER UP, AMANDA. YOU'VE WANTED THAT TOP FOR AGES. NOW YOU'VE GOT IT, THE LEAST YOU COULD DO IS SMILE.
I'M SORRY, MUM. I KNOW I'M BEING A REAL GRUMP, BUT I JUST CAN'T HELP IT.
LITTER

COME ON, LET'S GO FOR A HAMBURGER AND YOU CAN TELL ME ALL ABOUT IT.
OKAY.
MUM'S BEING REALLY KIND, BUT I DON'T THINK TALKING TO HER IS GOING TO HELP.

And—
YOU STILL HAVEN'T TOLD ME HOW YOU GOT ON WITH FIONA THE OTHER NIGHT. I HOPED YOU TWO MIGHT BE FRIENDS.
HUH! SHE SPENT THE WHOLE EVENING FLIRTING WITH THE BOYS — IT WAS REALLY EMBARRASSING. ANYWAY, WE HAD A FIGHT, AND SHE SAID SHE NEVER WANTED TO SEE ME AGAIN.

OH, AMANDA — I'M SURE SHE DIDN'T MEAN IT. WHY DON'T YOU GO ROUND TOMORROW AND TELL HER YOU STILL WANT TO BE FRIENDS?
I **CAN'T** DO THAT, MUM. SHE'D THINK I WAS SOFT.

But Mum insisted—
HELLO — IS FIONA IN?
I'M SORRY, AMANDA, YOU'VE JUST MISSED HER. SHE'S GONE OUT TO THE PICTURES WITH HER NEW BOYFRIEND, SIMON.

SO FIONA'S GOING OUT WITH SIMON. WELL, I NEVER FANCIED HIM ANYWAY, SO WHY SHOULD I CARE?

E265 LYF
OH, HECK. I **DO** CARE — IN FACT, I'M JEALOUS, EVEN THOUGH I'VE NO RIGHT TO BE. KATHY AND I ALWAYS SAID BOYS WEREN'T IMPORTANT, BUT I'M BEGINNING TO FEEL LIKE THEY'RE VERY IMPORTANT INDEED.

And—
CAN I ASK YOU A QUESTION, MUM? DO YOU THINK BOYS ARE IMPORTANT?
THAT'S SOMETHING YOU HAVE TO DECIDE FOR YOURSELF, LOVE. IS THERE ONE SPECIAL BOY?

NOT REALLY — AT LEAST I DIDN'T THINK HE WAS SPECIAL TILL HE STARTED GOING OUT WITH SOMEONE ELSE. NOW I'M NOT SO SURE.
IT'S JIM, ISN'T IT? I COULD TELL HE WAS VERY TAKEN WITH YOU.

NO, IT ISN'T JIM — HE ONLY SPEAKS TO ME BECAUSE I'M A FRIEND OF KATHY'S.
ARE YOU SURE? IT DOESN'T LOOK THAT WAY TO ME.

WHAT DOES SHE MEAN BY THAT? AND WHY'S LIFE SO COMPLICATED? EVERYTHING WAS MUCH SIMPLER WHEN KATHY WAS HERE.

Kathy's next letter was a surprise—

"DEAR AMANDA, YOU'LL NEVER GUESS WHAT — I'VE GOT A BOYFRIEND. HIS NAME'S BRUCE AND HE'S THE MOST GORGEOUS HUNK IN THE WORLD . . ."

I DON'T BELIEVE IT. KATHY ALWAYS SAID SHE WOULDN'T HAVE A BOYFRIEND TILL SHE WAS AT LEAST 15!

At school—

SIMON AND FIONA SEEM TO BE ENJOYING THEMSELVES. ALL I'VE DONE ALL DAY IS READ KATHY'S LETTER OVER AND OVER AGAIN.
HI, AMANDA.

OH! YOU GAVE ME A FRIGHT, JIM. DON'T YOU DARE SNEAK UP ON ME LIKE THAT AGAIN.
I'M SORRY — I JUST WANTED TO ASK IF THAT WAS A LETTER FROM KATHY YOU WERE READING.

WHAT IF IT IS? IT'S NONE OF YOUR BUSINESS!
HUH! SORRY I SPOKE.
WHY AM I BEING SO BAD TEMPERED? I PROMISED MYSELF I'D BE NICER TO PEOPLE, BUT I'M STILL SNAPPING ALL THE TIME.

That night—
"DEAR KATHY, I MISS YOU AND I'M JEALOUS THAT YOU'VE GOT A BOYFRIEND. I'M SO MISERABLE I CAN'T THINK STRAIGHT.

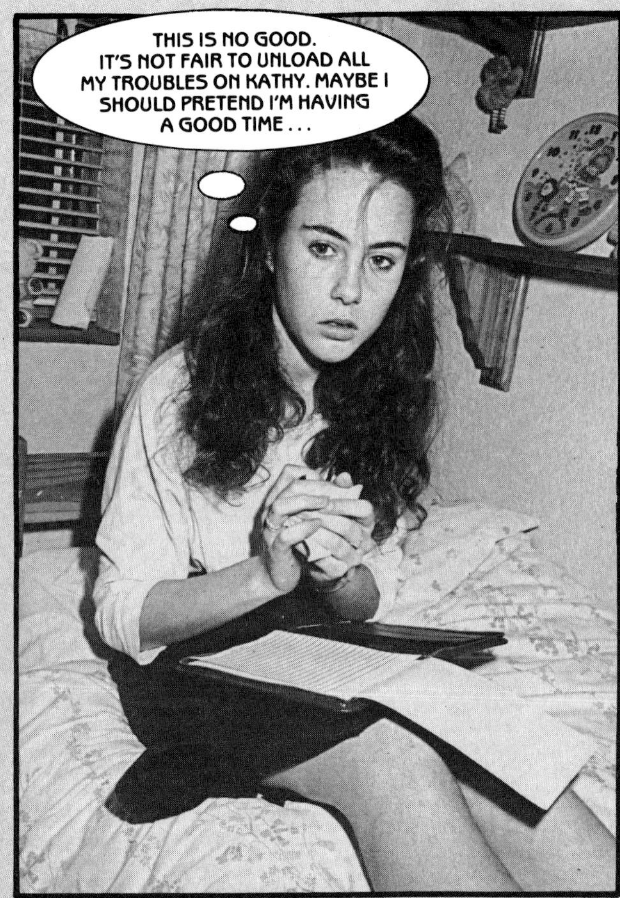

THIS IS NO GOOD. IT'S NOT FAIR TO UNLOAD ALL MY TROUBLES ON KATHY. MAYBE I SHOULD PRETEND I'M HAVING A GOOD TIME . . .

So—
". . . AND SINCE I'VE BEEN GOING OUT WITH JIM, I'VE NEVER BEEN HAPPIER." MAYBE I SHOULDN'T HAVE WRITTEN THAT BIT — BUT I HAD TO MAKE IT BELIEVABLE.

BESIDES, MUM'S SURE HE LIKES ME — AND I'VE DECIDED I LIKE HIM, TOO. NOW, DO I HAVE THE COURAGE TO DO SOMETHING ABOUT IT?

She did—
. . . SO I'D LIKE TO BUY YOU A COKE TO MAKE UP FOR BEING RUDE. WE COULD MEET AT THE CAFE!

IT'S NICE OF YOU TO ASK, AMANDA, BUT I'M GOING THROUGH TO HOLARTON TODAY — TO VISIT MY NEW GIRLFRIEND.

OH, I SEE. WELL, 'BYE, JIM.
I'VE MISSED MY CHANCE AGAIN — AND IT'S ALL MY OWN FAULT. SUDDENLY I'M LOSING ALL MY FRIENDS!

continued on page 106

"Hi!" takes a light-hearted look at young "love".

We've got a sneaky feeling that you're all a bunch of man-eaters out there, but just to be sure, you'd better answer these revealing questions.

MAN-MANIA

1. When you find out a boy fancies you, you:
a) Are flattered if a little embarrassed.
b) Add him to your list under 'H' for 'Hopefuls'.
c) Don't believe it — no one fancies *you.*

2. The best boyfriend to have is:
a) Nice looking, totally in love with you and has plenty of cash.
b) A good laugh when you're together and is sweet and thoughtful.
c) Don't know — haven't had any.

3. It's the disco tomorrow night and offers are coming in thick and fast. You go with:
a) The one everyone else would like to go with.
b) Anyone really.
c) The one you like best.

4. One of your friend's boyfriends is showing you a lot of attention. You:
a) Are flattered — but ignore it.
b) Love it!
c) Think he's probably taking the mick.

5. The way you dress is important because:
a) You like to be trendy and comfortable.
b) You hate not blending in and like to be the same as everyone else.
c) You have to get noticed, 'specially by all the BOYS.

6. Your boyfriend can't make it to the disco tonight 'cos he's ill. You:
a) Phone for a replacement.
b) Go with your pals.
c) Rush round with thermometer in hand.

7. The best thing in "Hi!" mag (spoilt for choice — Ed) is:
a) All the fantastic features.
b) Pin-ups of hunky *boys!*
c) The lovey-dovey stories.

8. Tonight's a big date — and you've just developed a huge spot on your nose.
a) Mega-disaster time — you may not be the star attraction.
b) Hey-ho, out with the cover stick — he'll just have to like you as you are!
c) Cancel and stay home — it's a good excuse.

9. A new girl in the class is getting all the attention. You:
a) Warn her that all the boys are total idiots — so she doesn't go out with them and they all still fancy you.
b) Laugh at them trying to impress her — but secretly wish you were her.
c) Hope your boyfriend doesn't fancy her.

10. Would you ask a boy out?
a) No — he'd just refuse.
b) Maybe — if you thought he was too shy to ask you.
c) Certainly not — they always ask you.

Now add up your score and read the conclusions

1) a-2, b-3, c-1
2) a-3, b-2, c-1
3) a-3, b-1, c-2
4) a-2, b-3, c-1
5) a-2, b-1, c-3
6) a-3, b-2, c-1
7) a-2, b-3, c-1
8) a-3, b-2, c-1
9) a-3, b-1, c-2
10) a-1, b-2, c-3

10-15

It appears we were wrong in your case, matey. You're about as much a man-eater as a pet gerbil! Bit of a lack of confidence here!

16-25

Yes — you definitely have the makings of a true man-eater. All you have to do now is make sure *you* don't actually fall for anyone yourself.

25-30

A fully-fledged out-and-out heart-breaker is what you are, and boy, do we pity the poor unsuspecting males who fall for you!

Special Prose Story

THE VALLEY GIRLS

WHAT do you do when your best mate's hopelessly in love and she needs your help? You help, right? Well, don't. Take it from me — it can land you in a whole heap of trouble. Look what happened to me . . . Oh, this is Kay here, by the way — Kay Newman. I live on the Valley estate, and so do my best friends, Zoe, Bev and lovestruck Linda. But to get to the point.

The trouble all started when Linda clapped eyes on Darren Heatley, that new boy in the fifth year. It was love at first sight. I mean, the rest of us didn't think he was anything special. Tallish, average-looking, I suppose — but hardly your Matt or Luke. But straight away, Linda had stars in her eyes.

"Ooh, Kay — isn't he FABBY? He's just a total DREAM!" she gasped.

Now, I only get dreams like that if I've eaten cheese for supper, but I didn't like to say so, 'cause I could see she'd got it bad. In fact, she'd got it so bad that two days later she was begging me to join an aerobics class with her. She'd found out his sister Janet was in it.

I got the picture. Get pally with the sister, get to know the brother. "Come off it," I protested. "Can you see me in an aerobics class?"

"Oh, please, Kay! Be a mate. I don't want to join alone . . ."

So we joined. Actually, the class wasn't bad, and Linda managed to position herself near Janet Heatley. She kept smiling brightly at her, but I could see she wasn't getting much response. Janet looked like one of those superkeen sporty types — only interested in the workout.

It was pretty hard work, too! It stretched muscles I didn't know I even had! Halfway through the session I was worn out, and by the end of it all I was fit for was to crawl home and collapse into a hot bath. I felt like I'd run twenty miles in clogs!

But Linda was dead bright and chirpy.

"What's with you?" I groaned. "I didn't notice your plan working."

That's where I was wrong. Linda had overheard Janet telling a friend of hers that her brother was dead keen on football and had just got into the school team . . . I should've seen what was coming, but I didn't.

Next day in school, as I hobbled along the corridor on stiff, aching legs, Linda rushed up and grabbed me.

"Kay, I've checked on the notice board. There's a football match tonight. If we go along and cheer, Darren's bound to notice me!" she beamed.

Notice that "we?"

She tucked her arm through mine. "Oh, go on, Kay. I couldn't go and watch the match alone! I'd feel a right wally."

"Oh, okay," I sighed. Honestly, the things you do for a pal!

I hadn't heard the weather forecast that day, had I? At quarter to four, we traipsed to the football pitch, at ten to four, Linda almost swooned at the sight of Darren's hairy legs as the teams trotted out on to the field.

And at four o'clock, the heavens opened.

We stuck it for ten minutes before they called the match off, by which point we were soaked to the skin. But Linda was quite happy. She claimed that as the teams ran off the pitch, Darren had looked straight at her.

I bet he had. He was probably trying to work out who the heck the two drowned rats were!

The next day, Linda got another brilliant bloke-grabbing plan. We were in town when who should we see but Guess-Who, going into the roller rink. Linda grabbed me and started following, with a determined look in her eye.

"Hey, wait!" I protested. "I can't — I'm skint . . ."

"I'LL pay us in. Oh, come on, Kay. You can't abandon a friend in need, can you?"

"Yes," I said, but she wasn't listening.

Before I knew it, we were kitted up with skates and on the rink, and Linda was dragging me past Darren, giving him her widest smile.

He smiled back at us. Linda was so excited, she giggled nervously and gave me a dig in the ribs — and I sat down. Hard.

"Ooh, sorry," she said as she picked me up. "But he smiled at me. He really DID! He's just soooooo gorgeous!"

"Good for you," I groaned, wondering how much more I was going to suffer before Darren Heatley wised up and asked her out.

But after about twenty minutes, he left the rink — and he STILL hadn't even spoken to her.

Linda handed our skates back to the guy in the ticket booth and we set off home. Secretly, I was hoping she'd give up on Darren — but when I sneaked a look at her, she was still smiling and dreamy, with those stars in her eyes.

Something had to be done. I mean, I couldn't take much more. So I got Zoe and Bev together, and the three of us worked out a brilliant plan.

I was the one who sneaked into the fifth form cloakroom and slipped the note into Darren's jacket.

MEET ME IN MARIO'S AT 7.30 — AN ADMIRER. XXX

"Ooh, it's so romantic," sighed Bev.

Then we grabbed Linda.

"Your dream has come true," I announced. "You go along to Mario's pizzeria tonight, 7.30, and HE will be waiting for you."

"Who?" asked Linda.

"Dreamboat! Loverboy! Darren Heatley! Who did you think — Mario?" I yelled.

"Oh — HIM?" said Linda casually. "No, thanks. I've gone off Darren Heatley."

"WHAT?" we shrieked.

Would you believe it? It turned out when she'd taken the skates back, the guy in the ticket booth had given her a big smile and a wink — and he's a DEAD ringer for Matt Goss. Tall, blond, blue eyes . . .

"Kay,"Linda wheedled. "You WILL come skating with me tonight, won't you? PLE-E-EASE?"

"No," I said glumly. "I've got something else to do tonight — thanks to you!"

Well, I couldn't just leave Darren to turn up at Mario's and find no one there, could I? He'd think it was all a rotten joke — and I felt I owed him some sort of an explanation.

So here I am. It's 7.25. I'm outside Mario's and I'm wishing I'd never tried to help Linda. What the heck am I going to say to Darren?

Oh, no . . . here he comes . . . This is it . . . HELP!

"Hi." He's taking the note out of his pocket. "It's Kay, isn't it? You know, I was sort of hoping the, er — admirer might be you."

WHAT?

Darren's smiling. He's got a nice smile . . .

"I've seen you around quite a bit lately," he says. "Saw you near our cloakroom today, too . . . that's why I turned up tonight. Fancy a pizza?"

Suddenly I notice what fab eyes he's got. Really deep, dark hazel brown . . .

I take back all I said. I'm glad I helped Linda out with her love life. I've a feeling that all the hassle might just be worth it . . . !

JILL'S PHOTO FILE

Dear Jill,

My best friend's boyfriend is a real rat — the trouble is I fancy him rotten! He flirts with me all the time and although he's really horrible to my mate I just can't help being attracted to him. Last Saturday he asked me to go out with him behind Tracey's back . . .

WHAT HAVE I DONE? I FANCY JAMIE, BUT I CAN'T GO OUT WITH HIM, CAN I?

Jill says,

It's always very flattering when someone asks you out, but do you really want to ruin a friendship because of this boy? He's not being fair to his girlfriend (your friend!) and I doubt very much whether he'd be very fair to you, either. Is it really worth losing a good friend over this boy? My advice to you is to put this boy firmly in his place.

SO I WON'T BE GOING OUT WITH YOU AT THE WEEKEND AND IF YOU DON'T STOP PESTERING ME I'LL TELL TRACEY WHAT'S GOING ON.

OKAY! OKAY! DON'T GET EXCITED — I ONLY ASKED!

Next day—

TRACEY, IS SOMETHING WRONG?
IT'S JAMIE. I SAW HIM LAST NIGHT — KISSING MANDY WALKER! AND WHEN HE SAW ME HE JUST LAUGHED!

NEVER MIND, TRACEY — YOU'VE STILL GOT ME. I'LL SOON CHEER YOU UP. WHO NEEDS BOYS?
THANKS, JULIE. I'M GLAD YOU'RE MY FRIEND.

I'M SO GLAD I MADE THE RIGHT DECISION. IT'S MUCH NICER TO HAVE A FRIEND LIKE TRACEY THAN A TWO-TIMING RAT LIKE JAMIE.

Lucy Paul and Lucy Young (confused? Let's just call them LP and LY) are both thirteen and they wrote and told us they were the very best of friends. We just had to track them down and have a chat. We met them in Walker's Café in Newcastle.

WHERE DID YOU FIRST MEET?
LP: We met at school — in the pre-first year at our school called 1L — and we just didn't like each other. LY had a big mouth and kept whispering to her best friend.
LY: Later in the first year we became good friends. One day we got the bus together, hit it off, and started getting the bus together every day. Then we both went on holiday to the Lake District and we've gone every year since.

WHAT DO YOU LIKE MOST ABOUT EACH OTHER?
LP: We've got the same sense of humour.
LY: We share problems and help each other out. We just do everything together.

WHAT ANNOYS YOU MOST ABOUT EACH OTHER?
LY: LP can be a bit unreliable, and she bends her fingers back until they crack. (YUCK!)
LP: She's loud, but then we're both loud really.

WHAT'S THE BEST AND MOST HORRIBLE THING SHE WEARS?
LP: She looks great in her cream skirt with her black polo shirt and dinner jacket. She looks terrible in really tight skirts. But she doesn't wear those any more.
LY: Her black and white spotty flares are terrific, especially with her black off-the-shoulder top. She had a really horrible pink and white stripey dress but she's thrown it out — thank goodness!

DO YOU EVER FALL OUT?
LP: About once every six months, I suppose. Perhaps we just get sick of each other. For example, this girl lied to me and there was a misunderstanding about another girl and her boyfriend, and Lucy believed the other girl, and not me!
LY: We always fall out over really stupid things.

WHAT DO YOU THINK OF EACH OTHER'S TASTE IN BOYS?
LP: We mostly agree, although sometimes we clash. For me they've got to be tall, dark, with a good personality and a good sense of humour. Good clothes are important, especially shoes. No trainers or track suits allowed.
LY: I feel just the same. But they don't necessarily have to be tall because that would rule out, well you promise you won't tell anybody . . . giggle, giggle, giggle . . . no, I can't tell you!

WHO ARE YOUR FAVOURITE POP STARS?
LP: Wet Wet Wet.
LY: Wet Wet Wet are great, especially Marti Pellow. We went to see them in concert.
LP: Nathan from Brother Beyond is nice.
LY: But we just like him — not their music! Yazz is good too, and Erasure.
LP: Perfect Day are good.
LY: I like Breathe too.
LP: Then Jerico are brill, but they haven't done anything for ages.

WHO WOULD YOU MOST LIKE TO LOOK LIKE IF YOU HAD THE CHOICE?
LP: Any model would do! I wouldn't mind looking like Marilyn Monroe (wouldn't we all?)!
LY: There's a girl that gets my train, and I'd love to look like her. She's the exact opposite of me. She has brown hair, dark skin and she's thin — sort of continental looking.

DO YOU SHARE THE SAME HOBBIES?
LY: Definitely.
LP: Yes, discos, boys and music!!

ANY FUNNY STORIES ABOUT EACH OTHER?
LP: We do daft things all the time.
LY: We lie about our ages all the time.
LP: And we flirt on holiday!

WHAT DO YOU USUALLY DO TO PASS THE TIME?
LY: We pass a lot of time on the phone. My mum thinks it's too much!
LP: We go into town every Saturday to meet friends and we go to as many parties as possible.

DO YOU THINK YOU'LL ALWAYS BE FRIENDS?
LY: Definitely. We're just really well-suited.
LP: Even if we do fall out we will always get back together. It's usually me that makes the first move.

IF YOU COULD CHANGE ONE THING ABOUT EACH OTHER WHAT WOULD IT BE?
LP: Lucy bites her nails really badly. That's the only thing I'd change about her.
LY: I wouldn't change anything. I like her the way she is.

WHAT MAKES A PERFECT BEST FRIEND?
LP: My definition would be: Someone with a good personality able to take a joke, a lot of fun, and with whom you share the same interests.
LY: And someone you can discuss your problems with. Like Lucy.
LP: Lucy listens to me more than I listen to her. I usually listen and then go and do the opposite when she gives me advice. Lucy takes more notice of my advice.

WOULD BOYFRIENDS EVER CAUSE A PROBLEM IN YOUR RELATIONSHIP?
LP: We would never let a boyfriend come between the two of us — it's as simple as that. We like each other too much. We'd always consult each other before arranging something which would cause problems.
LY: Boys cause problems all the time, through simple things. Lucy fancied a boy for two years and told me he was going to ask her out. But he didn't at first — it took ages. Finally he got down on one knee at a disco and asked her out. It caused a real stir!

Me and my best friend

JUST A MINI!

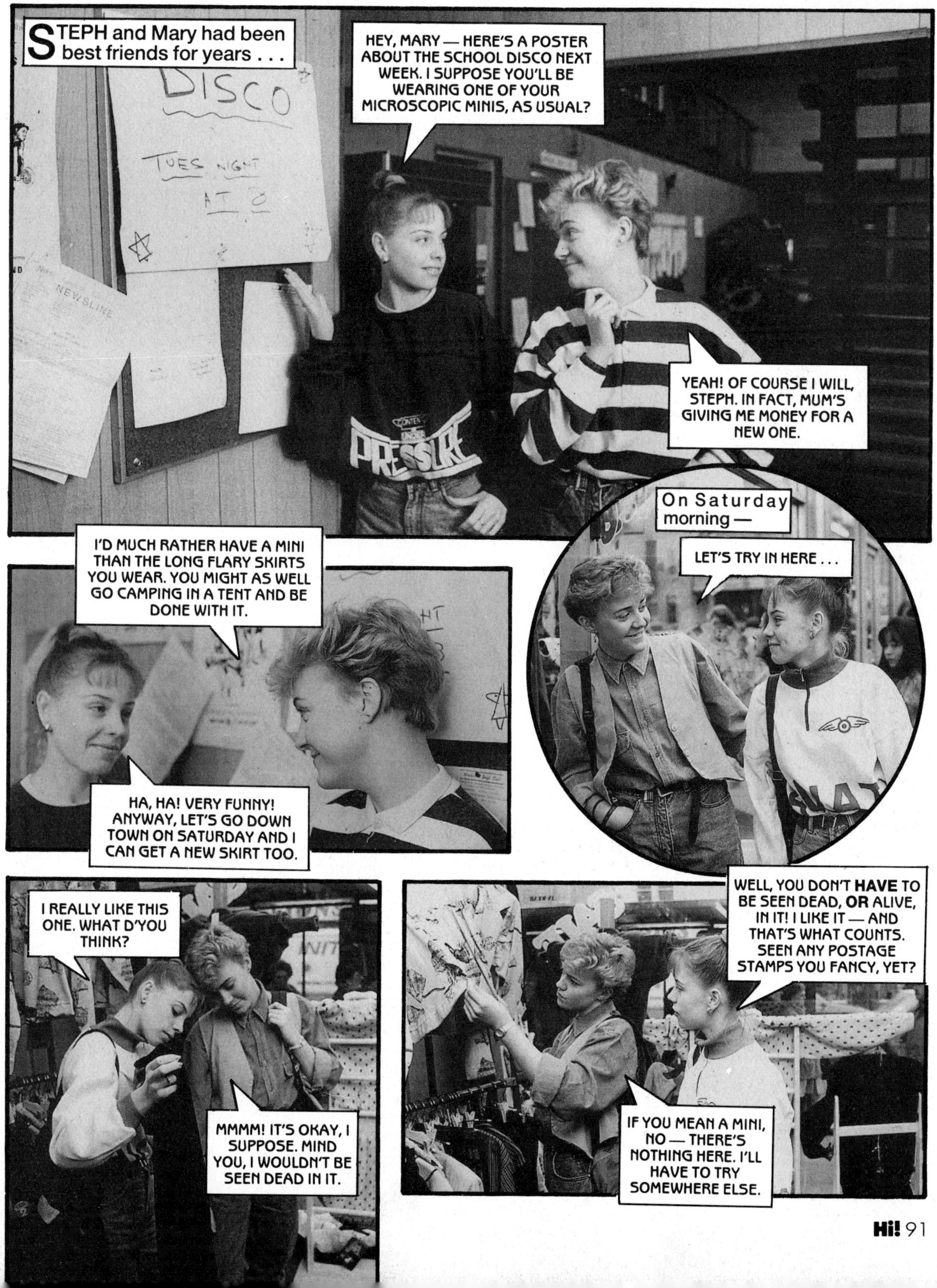

STEPH and Mary had been best friends for years . . .

HEY, MARY — HERE'S A POSTER ABOUT THE SCHOOL DISCO NEXT WEEK. I SUPPOSE YOU'LL BE WEARING ONE OF YOUR MICROSCOPIC MINIS, AS USUAL?

YEAH! OF COURSE I WILL, STEPH. IN FACT, MUM'S GIVING ME MONEY FOR A NEW ONE.

I'D MUCH RATHER HAVE A MINI THAN THE LONG FLARY SKIRTS YOU WEAR. YOU MIGHT AS WELL GO CAMPING IN A TENT AND BE DONE WITH IT.

HA, HA! VERY FUNNY! ANYWAY, LET'S GO DOWN TOWN ON SATURDAY AND I CAN GET A NEW SKIRT TOO.

On Saturday morning —

LET'S TRY IN HERE . . .

An hour later —
THIS ONE'S NOT BAD — BUT I'M NOT SURE ABOUT THE STRIPES . . .
OH, FOR GOODNESS' SAKE, MAKE UP YOUR MIND OR WE'LL BE HERE ALL DAY!

MMMM — I'M STILL NOT SURE IF I LIKE IT!
LOOKS OKAY — FOR A MINI! MAYBE IT'S YOUR LEGS YOU DON'T LIKE.

WHAT D'YOU MEAN BY THAT? THERE'S NOTHING WRONG WITH MY LEGS.
WELL MINE ARE ACHING. I'M SICK OF TRAILING AROUND ALL THESE SHOPS AFTER YOU.

I'M SORRY YOU'VE BEEN BORED. WHY DON'T YOU GO HOME AND TRY ON YOUR TENT.
DON'T WORRY — I'M GOING!

THAT'S THE FIRST TIME WE'VE EVER FALLEN OUT OVER CLOTHES — BUT WHO CARES? OH, THIS SKIRT LOOKS JUST RIGHT. I'LL BUY IT.

And—
YOUR NEW MINI'S NICE, LOVE, BUT WHERE'S STEPH? I THOUGHT SHE WAS COMING BACK HERE WITH YOU.
ER — NOT TODAY, MUM — SHE'S BUSY.
BUSY SULKING!

On Monday —
STEPH'S STILL IN THE HUFF — ALL OVER OUR STUPID SKIRTS! WELL, SHE CAN BE LIKE THAT IF SHE WANTS — IT'S NO SKIN OFF MY NOSE.

On Tuesday night—
IT'S THE DISCO TONIGHT AND WE STILL HAVEN'T SAID A WORD TO EACH OTHER. NOW I'LL HAVE TO GO ON MY OWN. I'D RATHER GO WITH JANE BUT WHY SHOULD I BE THE FIRST TO SAY SORRY.

I LEANED AGAINST OUR NEWLY-PAINTED GARAGE DOOR AND GOT PAINT MARKS ON MY LONG SKIRT. MUM HAD TO CUT THE BOTTOM BIT OFF.

AND I'VE GOT BANDAGED KNEES, SO I HAD TO WEAR THIS LONG SKIRT TO COVER THEM UP. OH, STEPH! THIS IS A HOOT!

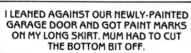

POP THE QUESTION

Some tough questions on your favourite popsters. Get ready for some brain strain!

Nothing But The Truth?

1. A great Bon Jovi album was "You'll Fall When It Rains". True or False?

2. Samantha Fox's hit "I Only Wanna Be With You" was also a hit for Dusty Springfield in the 60s. True or False?

3. Patrick Swayze's not a bad singer. True or False?

4. Carol Decker from T'Pau once trained to be a female astronaut. True or False?

5. Simon Mayo's real name is Simon Mayonnaise, but he was so embarrassed by this surname that he shortened it. True or False?

6. Michael Hutchence is actually the ONLY member of INXS. He dresses up to look like the others. True or False?

7. A new group is causing an enormous fuss in the U.S.A. They're called The Groovy Foxes and Michael J. Fox is the lead guitarist. True or False?

8. Tiffany's real name is Jane Smith. True or False?

9. Jermaine Stewart is Michael Jackson's secret half-brother. True or False?

10. Whitney Houston once earned thousands of dollars as a model before turning to singing as a career. True or False?

POP IN A BOX

Here's a mega crossword for you to sweat over. No peeking at the answers, though 'cos we'll be MAD!

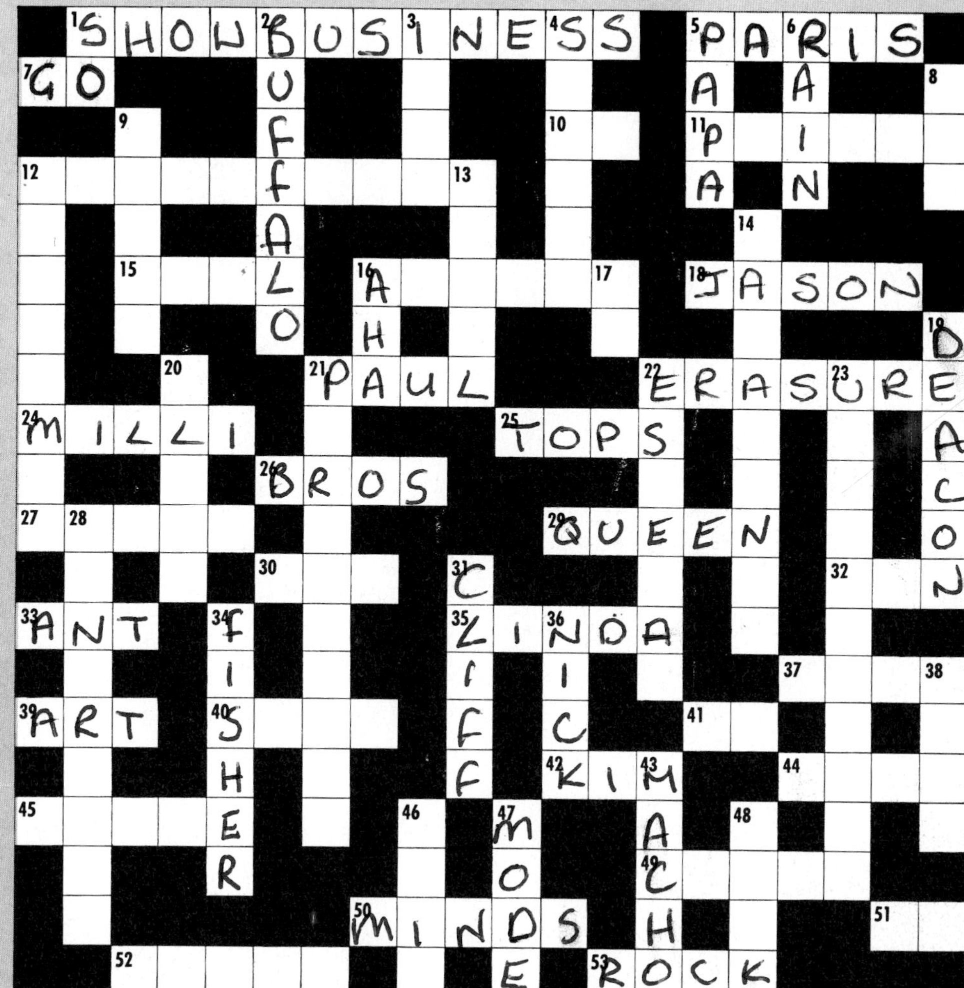

ACROSS

1. A video from The Pets (12)
5. Mica's surname — the capital of France (5)
7. -- West — two hit wonders? (2)
10. - & -, Breathe's record label (1, 1)
11. He likes his friends to call him Christopher (6)
12. Chris Duffy and Phil Cilia make up this watery group (10)
15. L. L. ---- J. — romantic rapper (4)
16. See 9 down
18. Mr Donovan the Aussie Hunk (5)
21. Ex-Beatle McCartney (ask your mum!) (4)
22. Andy Bell is one half of this group (7)
24. ----- Vanilli — a gruesome twosome! (5)
25. They went 'Loco In Acapulco' — The Four ---- (4)
26. The Goss boys and Craig (4)
27. Whitney Houston is this relation to Dionne Warwick (5)
29. Ageing 'royal' popsters (5)
30. You could get a boxed --- of Bruce Springsteen records! (3)
32. A house group --- City (3)
33. His first name's Adam and he used to dress up as a highwayman! (3)
35. Hue and Cry were 'Looking For -----' at the beginning of '89 (5)
37. A surprise duo, Marc Almond and ---- Pitney (4)
39. --- of Noise (3)
40. Sultry singer — DASE (4)
41. Disc Jockey in short (1, 1)
42. She's Wilde! (3)
44. ----, Truth and Honesty — a Nanas hit (4)
45. Mr Clarke, the other half of 22 across (5)
49. ----- Datchler — ex Johnny Hates Jazz (5)
50. Jim Kerr and company, members of a Simple group (5)
51. Extended Play — shortened! (1, 1)
52. Mr Johnson, ex-leader of Frankie's Hollywood gang (5)
53. ---- 'n' Roll! (4)

DOWN

1. Peter Gabriel's 'Sledgehammer' of an album! (2)
2. and 4 down. Neneh Cherry's first hit (7, 6)
3. Heavy metal Maiden (4)
4. See 2 down.
5. Wee ---- Girl Rappers (4)
6. '---- Town' an album by 19 down (4)
8. Mick Hucknall's group are Simply this colour (3)
9. 16 across and 12 down. They are the Hit Factory (5, 6, 8)
12. See 9 down.
13. Bonnie Tyler had a '----- Eclipse of the Heart' (5)
14. Their first hit was 'Tribute' (9)
16. Morten, Mags and Pal (3)
17. 'It's -- Secret' — a track on Kylie's album (2)
19. A BLUE group (6)
20. Colin Vernacombe's dark name (5)
21. Mark, Woody, Kevin and Scotty are the members of this group (7, 3)
22. Gloria's Miami Sound Machine (7)
23. His Purpleness and Sheena Easton had this hit single together (1, 3, 3, 4)
28. They had a 'Good Life'! (5, 4)
31. Mr Richard had a Christmas hit with 'Mistletoe and Wine' (5)
34. Climie's other half (6)
36. ---- Heyward (4)
38. Get this Brother Beyond album (4)
43. Sinitta's 'Toy Boy' has to be so ----- (5)
46. These record industry awards were a shambles this year (4)
47. Depeche ---- (4)
48. '---- This Way' Run DMC and Aerosmith told us (4)

ANSWERS TO – POP IN A BOX.

ACROSS

1. Showbusiness 5. Paris 7. Go 10. A&M 11. Prince 12. Waterfront 15. Cool 16. Aitken 18. Jason 21. Paul 22. Erasure 24. Milli 25. Tops 26. Bros 27. Niece 29. Queen 30. Set 32. Ten 33. Ant 35. Linda 37. Gene 39. Art 40. Sade 41. D.J. 42. Kim 44. Love 45. Vince 49. Clark 50. Minds 51.EP 52. Holly 53.Rock

DOWN

1. So 2. Buffalo 3. Iron 4. Stance 5. Papa 6. Rain 8. Red 9. Stock 12. Waterman 13. Total 14. Pasadenas 16. A-ha 17. No 19. Deacon 20. Black 21. Perfect Day 22. Estefan 23. U Got The Look 28. Inner City 31. Cliff 34.Fisher 36. Nick 38. Even 43. Macho 46. Brit 47. Mode 48. Walk.

ANSWERS TO – POP THE QUESTION.

1. False — "Slippery When Wet". 2. True. 3. True — well he did have a hit with "She's Like The Wind". 4. False. 5. False. 6. False — well, he won't admit it anyway! 7. False — we hope! 8. False — it's Tiffany Darwisch. 9. False — although they do both have squeaky voices! 10. True.

A Week With Liz

MONDAY

Slept in! Woke up at 9.25 am — was supposed to be at work for nine! Bought the Ed a Twirl on the way to work to try to soften her up — without success! She took the Twirl and STILL gave me a telling off for being late! Hmmmph! I was tempted to sabotage her coffee when she sent me to the canteen, but I chickened out! I'm too young to die!!

TUESDAY

Slept in again! Bought the Ed two Twirls, but they didn't work either! Never mind, I escaped from the office this afternoon to help the Fashion Ed on a shoot. My job was to carry all the clothes and iron them ready for the models to wear. How was I to know the iron was going to over-heat? I only burnt the back and I'm sure a few pins would've hidden the — er — medium-sized burn in that extremely expensive T-shirt.

WEDNESDAY

I made sure I didn't sleep in THIS morning — I was up at the crack of dawn and in work by 8.30 am. Only trouble was by ten o'clock I had fallen asleep — and even worse I'd started snoring! I only woke up when I sensed someone standing over me — it was the Ed. Steam was coming out of her ears and I'm sure she would've pulverised me if I hadn't whipped out a Twirl and waved it in her face! Phew! The closest shave yet.

THURSDAY

Got stuck into your letters today — you're all crazy! The Ed thinks I'M mad, but you lot are much worse! Here's an example of some of your jokes —

What do you call a sheep with no legs?

— A cloud!

What do you call a deer with no eyes?

— No eye-deer! (No idea!)

What do you call a deer with no eyes and no legs?

— Still no eye-deer!

See what I mean?

FRIDAY

The best day of the week! The Ed was away to some important conference or other — actually I think she went shopping for new clothes, she's got LOADS of money! I spent most of the day chatting to the new hunk in the canteen. I don't think I impressed him too much — I spilt most of my coffee all over him! Well, it wasn't my fault — I didn't know someone was going to throw a chair into my path as I walked towards him!

Spent the rest of the day sulking 'cos my so-called friends in the "Hi!" office said they were going to tell the Ed on Monday that I hadn't done any work — tell-tales!

SATURDAY

Spent all day in bed. Well, a girl needs her beauty sleep, doesn't she?

SUNDAY

I'm sure I'm sickening for something. I just can't eat a thing! All right, so I ate that deep pan pizza, but if I hadn't eaten it today it would've gone off! And that box of Milk Tray was just cluttering up the living room!

Okay, I admit it — I'm scared to go to work tomorrow, but wouldn't you be? Where's that box of Twirls?

A READER'S TRUE STORY

She was my best friend — and I hurt her . . .

"SORRY-BUT IT'S TOO LATE . . ."

IT'S Friday evening, and on Fridays I always go to the Youth Club with Liz.

We've been going for nearly two years now — but we've been friends even longer than that.

I can still remember the day we met. I was in Mrs Timberlake's class and she brought in this new girl, Liz Fraser, and introduced her to us. I didn't actually take much notice at the time. I was best friends with Sara Potter — we went everywhere together. But soon after that, Sara and I fell out — and Liz asked me if I'd go around with her.

Liz and I soon became the best of friends. At school we were always together of course, but we spent all our free time with each other, too. Luckily, our houses were quite close, so she was always popping into mine or I was running down to hers. It was great!

Some years we even went on holiday with each other's families! Liz's folks took me to Torquay for a fortnight, and she came to North Wales with mine.

The Torquay holiday was the summer before we transferred to the comp. I remember how worried we both were that we might get split up and put into different classes there, but luckily we didn't!

If anything, we became even better friends. We seemed to be even closer than before and talked about everything — but now it wasn't "Sindy" dolls or "My Little Ponies" we discussed it was discos, pop music — and boys! We were both dreading and looking forward to our first date.

In the end it was me who was asked out first — by Mike, a boy in the year above ours. He took me to the pictures, and afterwards I told Liz all about it.

Mike and I dated for three weeks, but I was very careful not to forget about Liz during that time. We still spent all our time at school together — Mike preferred to be with his own friends then anyway, so that was fine. And Liz and I still saw each other in the evenings, plus we didn't miss our regular Friday trips to the Youth Club.

After three weeks, though, Mike and I finished. I was a bit upset at first, but Liz helped me to get over it.

For a few months, we went back to our usual routine — then it was Liz's turn to find a boyfriend. Tim was a boy who'd started coming to our Youth Club, and he got talking to Liz while I was playing in a table tennis competition one week, and he soon asked her out.

At the Youth Club they spent the time together, while I chatted to other people or took part in the activities. But Liz still always called round at my house first, so that we could at least walk to the club together.

But not tonight.

It's gone seven now and Liz hasn't come and she won't ever come again either.The friendship that we shared is over now. It's ruined. And it's all my fault.

It happened while Liz was away for a few days visiting her gran.

I was left at home on my own, bored, fed up and lonely. And when I met Tim in town and he invited me to go for a coffee, I just said yes . . .

One thing led to another, and before I knew what had happened, we'd moved on from the cafe to the park. Then we were standing under some trees and kissing . . .

We went out twice more after that before Liz came home. Of course I knew I shouldn't, but I just kept hoping Liz would understand. I even half convinced myself that she'd probably met someone new while she was away and wouldn't want Tim any more anyway.

But when Liz came back she did want him — in fact, she'd missed him a lot. And when she found out about me and Tim . . . well, she could hardly believe it.

We had a huge argument, which ended with Liz storming off and vowing never to speak to me again. So far, she hasn't. And I'm sure it'll stay that way — Liz always does exactly what she says.

Of course, I've still got Tim. But he dropped Liz quickly enough when it suited him, so I can't help thinking the same will happen to me — or I'll drop him. Already he's beginning to annoy me because he's late for dates, and hardly seems to notice I'm around some times.

He's not that special at all, I realise now. Yet, for him, I sacrificed my friendship with Liz. Everything we shared has gone, and it's all my fault.

I've learned too late that friends are more important than anything a boy has to offer . . .

TASTING!

1. DAIRY CRUNCH
2. BOOST
3. DOUBLE DECKER
4. TWIX
5. MARS BAR
6. WISPA
7. TOFFEE CRISP
8. TWIRL
9. WHITE TOBLERONE
10. MARATHON

ARE you a chocaholic? Can you tell your Mars Bar from your Marathon, your Twirl from your Twix? Blindfold at the ready, we asked some likely looking choccy addicts to taste ten chocolate bars and try to guess what they were. 'Snot as easy as you think! Here's what they said — in between chomps and slurps!

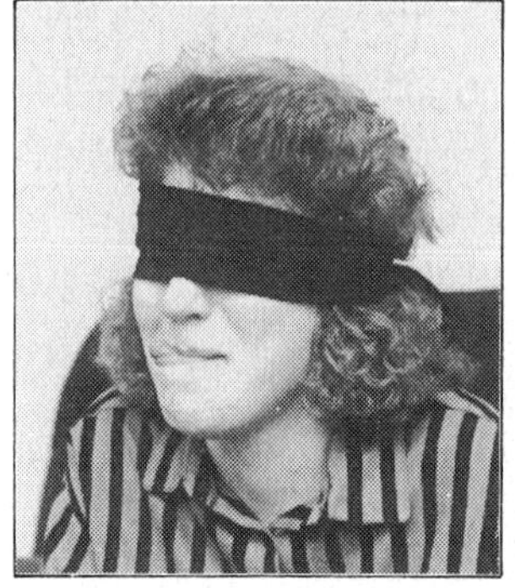

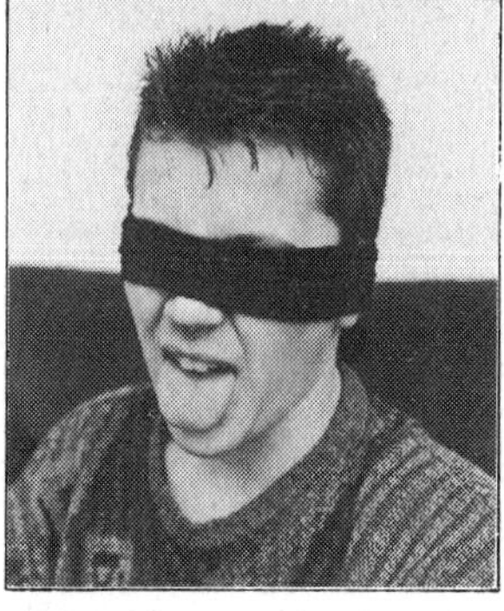

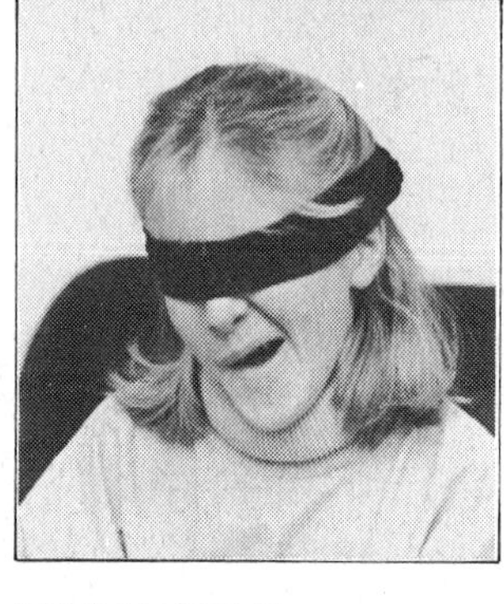

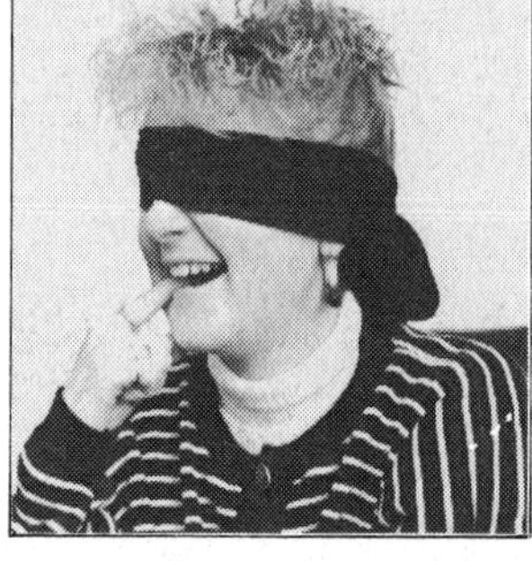

TANYA BERTHOUD
Fave choccy — Twix.

1. Rice crispy bits? Mm — it's scrummy! Chocolate Crunch — white . . . Dairy Crunch!
2. Toffee and coconut. Boost!
3. Hm — it's got a biscuity bit on the bottom . . . Double Decker.
4. Crispy with a creamy bit on the top. Quite nice. Don't know what it is . . . what? Twix? But that's my favourite!
5. Really chewy with a soft bit on top. Mars Bar.
6. Light and fluffy, like an Aero. A Wispa?
7. Crispies again. Could it be a Toffee Crisp?
8. Yum! Soft and crumbly and really nice. Twirl.
9. This is great too. It's got crunchy bits, but they're not nuts. A white Toblerone.
10. Peanuts — Marathon!

Chocaholic Rating 9/10.

RORY FRASER
Fave choccy — Yorkie.

1. Mm — chocolate and nuts. Erm . . . er . . . hum . . . ooh . . . I don't know!
2. This is difficult! Toffee or something. I've had it before, but I can't remember what it's called!
3. Kind of biscuity . . . and caramel . . . er . . . Double Decker!
4. Oh! Er . . . this is more like a Double Decker!
5. Mars Bar — that was easy!
6. Chocolate and — nothing! Wispa!
7. Crunchy — it's okay, I suppose. Wait — I know what it is (the suspense is killing us!). Toffee Crisp!
8. Nice — mm-mm! Flaky chocolate — a Twirl.
9. Don't like this much. In fact — YEURGH! Peanuts? Toffee 'n' stuff? Don't know.
10. Peanuts, this time. A marathon!

Chocaholic Rating 6/10.

KERI GRAHAM
Fave choccy — Yorkie.

1. Has it got wafer in it? (Hey — *we* ask the questions!) It's really nice. Oh, it's that one where the blinds shut on it in the advert and bite a bit off! It's white! And . . . (okay, okay — you can have it!)
2. Boost — just like that!
3. Toffee with biscuit in it. Has this got coconut in it too? Don't know.
4. Em — tastes of toffee. Erm — Munchies!
5. Doesn't have much of a taste. It's not as nice as some. Oh, yes — a Mars!
6. Soft — mmmmm (okay — get on with it!). Wispa!
7. This one's easy — Toffee Crisp.
8. Em — a bit like a Flake, but I think it's a Twirl.
9. Another easy-peasy one — Toblerone . . . white, I think.
10. Kind of chewy. Got raisins in it? Oh, nuts! Picnic? No . . . my mind's a blank!

Chocaholic Rating 7/10.

DAWN MITCHELL
Fave choccy — Whole Nut.

1. Mmm — really milky and crunchy. It's okay — nothing great. Is it that thing — Dairy Crunch? A white one.
2. Coconut something or other. Tastes a bit odd — don't like it and I don't know what it is.
3. (Lots of crunching noises!) Mm — I don't know. I should, 'cos I love chocolate!
4. Biscuit or something and caramel. A Trio or something? It's a Twix? I really like them too!
5. Very chewy! There's a bit stuck in my teeth! Is it a Caramel?
6. Oh — that's an Aero!
7. Haven't a clue! It's crunchy and chocolatey. A Crunchie!
8. A Flake? Oh, no — a Ripple!
9. Milky with little crunchy bits. The shape gives it away a bit. Toblerone!
10. Erm — sort of like a Mars Bar, but . . . different! Got crunchy bits on the top — oh, they're nuts! It's Topic!

Chocaholic Rating 2/10.

TASTING!

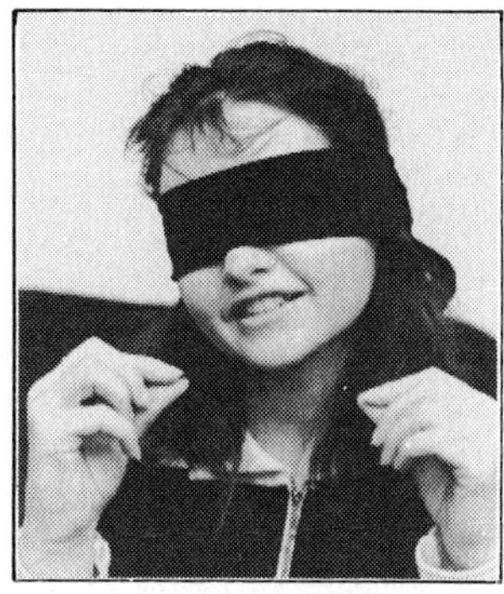

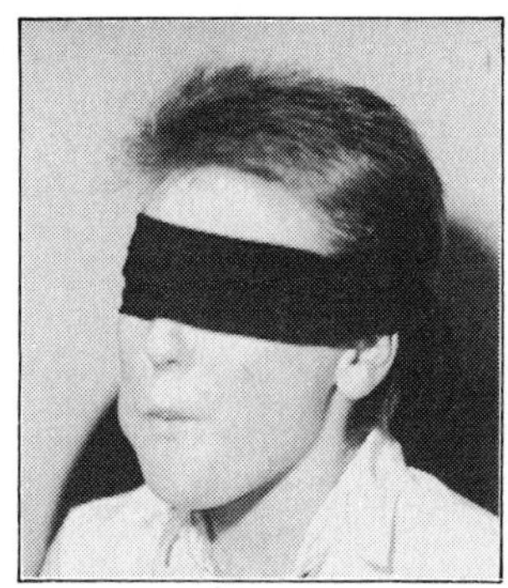

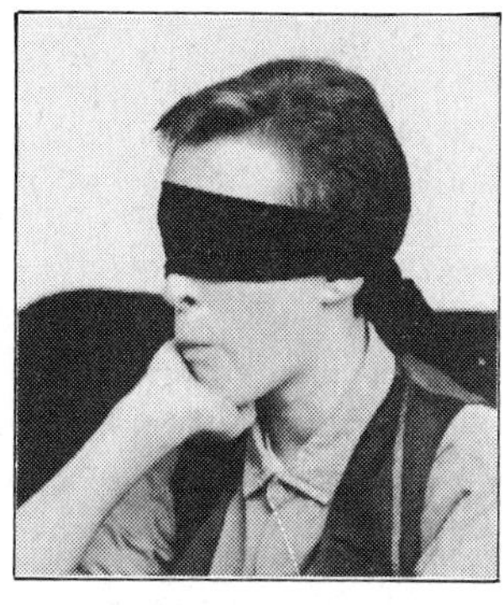

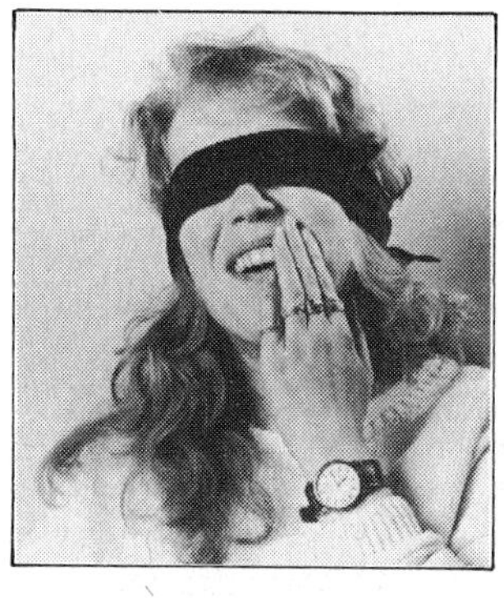

SARAH-JANE DUNCAN
Fave choccy — Milky Bar.

1. Crispy kind of stuff with nougatty bits. It's great! Em — Dairy Crunch . . . white!
2. Soft toffee, nice 'n' creamy. Got a coconut taste. Boost!
3. Very crunchy. Let me see . . . Double Decker.
4. Hmmm — smooth and toffee-ish with a crunchy bit. They come in those long packets and you get them in mint as well. I've got it! Munchies!
5. Ooh — I'm getting full! Erm — quite chewy. Mars, I think.
6. Crumbly. Just chocolate. Mmm — lovely — Wispa.
7. Don't like it very much — very crispy. Toffee Crisp?
8. Nice and crumbly — yummy taste. Twirl!
9. Ooh — it's really hard. Nuts and things. It's quite nice really — Whole Nut?
10. I'm really full now! Quite chewy. *This* has got nuts. Em — some sort of nutty bar. Don't know . . .

Chocolate Rating 7/10.

MANDY MONAGHAN
Fave choccy — Twirl.

1. Nice and crunchy. Mmm — it's got chocolate on it (No!). White Dairy Crunch!
2. Erm — giggle, giggle — really chewy! It sticks to your teeth. Coconut . . . Boost!
3. Crunchy and a bit chewy as well. Don't like it much. Crunchie?
4. Soft on top and crunchy underneath. Yum! Twix.
5. Mmm — this is really good. Soft and chewy . . . Milky Way?
6. Very tasty. Chocolate all the way through. Mmm — Aero . . .
7. Really crunchy. 'Sgot crispies in it. And toffee . . . don't like it. No idea what it is.
8. Mmm — luvverly! Quite crumbly — melts in your mouth. Flake . . . no! It's a Twirl — my favourite!
9. Not very nice. Eeugh! Bit sickening. White Toblerone.
10. Really nice — brilliant! Marathon.

Chocoaholic Rating 6/10.

PETER BANKS
Fave choccy — Galaxy.

1. It's like the Gold Bar . . . with caramel chocolate and biscuity bits — I think!
2. That's a Boost!
3. Chomp, chew! Toffee, caramel, crispy bits (eh, that's what he said about the first one — well, almost!) Don't like it much. Don't know what it is.
4. Twix!
5. Mmm — this is ace. Caramel and chocolate. But I don't know what it is!
6. Think I know this one, I'll whisper it — Wispa!
7. Er — not very keen on this. Is it a Toffee Crisp?
8. Bit like a Flake, but nicer. A Twirl.
9. This is an easy one — Toblerone — a white one.
10. Nuts (same to you!), caramel. It's a Marathon.

Chocahaolic Rating 7/10.

AND LAST BUT NOT LEAST . . . OUR OWN LOVELY LIZ!
Fave choccy — Milky Bar.

1. Slurp — White Dairy Crunch! That's my *2nd* favourite.
2. Yum — Boost!
3. Slooo — Double Decker!
4. Mmm — two for the price of one. Twix!
5. My 3rd favourite — Mars!
6. Drool! Wispa!
7. Toffee Crisp . . . More! More!
8. Ooh — maybe *this* is the best. Twirl!
9. White Toblerone! I've got expensive taste!
10. Yummy-yum! Marathon. What — is that all? Pass the Milky Bar!

Chocaholic Rating 10/10
(Quick — pass the diet sheet!)

THE Hi! A

The 'Where Are They Now Award'

We loved them, we screamed at them, we bought ALL their records — and then they disappeared! Who? Ben and Curiosity Killed The Cat, of course. Come back, boys!

The 'Girl We Would Most Like To Be' Award

She's slim, pretty — and she's got Jason Donovan (sort of!). Yes, it's Kylie Minogue! If she wasn't so nice, we'd hate her!

The 'Grumpiest Soap On TV' Award

No competition here — the unhappy inhabitants of Albert Square win hands down. Cheer up 'EastEnders' please, BBC.

Grumps, groans and fights galore!

The 'Crumbliest DJ On Radio 1' Award

Radio 1 seems to be full of crumblies (i.e. anyone over thirty) and "Hi!" couldn't decide which one is the oldest, so this award goes to Simon Bates, DLT, John Peel and Mike Read!

Ancient . . . . . . pretty old . . .

. . . crumbled . . .

The 'Oh Why Doesn't He Give Up' Award

He's not funny, and he can't dress! Who are we talking about? Timmy 'zany' Mallett, of course. Let's hope he gives up v. soon!

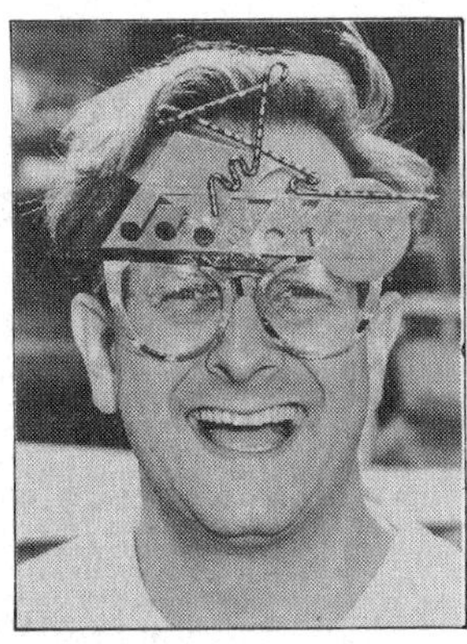

The 'Why Is It Still On TV When It's So Boring' Award

Tough decision here, but 'Blue Peter' wins — does anyone REALLY want to know how to make things out of empty cornflake packets?
Well, no, they don't, actually!
P.S. They're so awful, we're not even printing a photo of them — so there!

The 'Oh Why Isn't He A Bit Younger So We Could Fancy Him' Award

You know how it is, you'd REALLY like to fancy someone, but, well, they're a bit of a crumbly. And no one fits the bill better than balding Bruce Willis . . . if only he was ten (twenty?) years younger!

The 'My Goodness I Can't Believe What She's Wearing' Award

It's the girl with the longest legs in pop . . . Yazz! Who could forget the ballet tutu and the denim jacket — worn together! The gal's got style! (Sort of!)

The 'Best Magazine In The World' Award

We had a vote round the office for this one, and (blush, blush) "Hi!" got 100% of the votes! Hope you agree!

The 'Best Readers In The World' Award

This one goes to YOU — the best bunch of readers a magazine could have. Thanks a lot!

The 'Oh Why Doesn't He Ask Me Out' Award

There's a tie for this award — between Matt Bros, Michael J., River Phoenix, Jason Donovan . . . you can choose the winner for this one yourself!

SWITCHED

ARE YOU A SQUARE-EYED TELLY ADDICT? NOW'S YOUR CHANCE TO FIND OUT YOUR GOGGLE-BOX RATING!

QUICK QUIZ

Let's start with six easy questions, all about some of your favourite shows, past and present. Score 1 point for every one you get right.

1. No prizes for naming the Neighbour below — but can you remember what her mother was called?

2. In which American comedy can you see Jason Bateman?
3. Name Phillip Schofield's furry little friend.
4. What Blanche, Rose, Dorothy and Sophia are known as.
5. It's on every Thursday and introduces all the latest chart sounds.
6. Where do the Flintstones live?

SOAP SPOT

How much do you REALLY know about soaps? We've made these questions extra tough just to catch you out, so you can score 2 points for each one you get right.

1. Name EastEnder Dot Cotton's husband.
2. His tragic death by stabbing had lots of Brookie fans in tears. Who was he?
3. Which glamorous mum has children called Adam, Stephen, Fallon and Amanda?
4. In Coronation Street, what was the name of Jenny Bradley's French ex-fiance?
5. Which Aussie soap is set in a place called Wandin Valley?
6. Y'all know which U.S. city Dallas is set in. But can you name the 'county' where Southfork can be found?

MISSING LINK

Fill in the missing letters to find six T.V. quiz shows and score 1 point for each one.

1. A ----T--- Of Sport.
2. The -Y----- Game.
3. Going For -O--
4. ---- Us A -L--
5. Strike It ---K-
6. What's -Y --N-?

KIDS STUFF

Your little bruvs or sisters might be able to help you with some of these pre-school puzzles — and you can award yourself 2 points for every correct answer.

1. Who's the postman for the village of Greendale?
2. Where will you see Zippy, George and Bungle?
3. Who lived in a wicker basket with a teddy bear and a rag doll?
4. Which character started his adventures in a fancy dress shop?
5. On which programme did you look through a different shaped window every day?
6. Who were Pugh, Barney McGrew, Cuthbert, Dibble and Grubb?

IN THE FAMILY

These are SO easy, even the Ed knows the answers! All you have to do is name the shows these famous families appear in. 1 point for each.

1. The Boswells. 2. The Rogers. 3. The Huxtables.
4. The Keatons. 5. The Carringtons. 6. The Fletchers.

6. Well, two of them are!

ON!

ALL MIXED UP!

That's what these are — and there's 1 point for each question. Unscramble the letters to find six top T.V. shows.

1. ERNGGA ILLH.
2. NIGGO IVEL.
3. LIBDN ATED.
4. RKBULOTBCSES.
5. ORTMUHTOMO.
6. PEUSSRIR ERPRSSUI.

JUST FOR FUN

And finally, can you find the names of these twelve cartoon characters hidden in the wordsquare? They can read forwards, backwards, up, down or diagonally. No points for solving this — but you can deduct 2 for every name you DON'T find!

TOM, JERRY, POPEYE, OLIVE OYL, BUTCH, SYLVESTER, BUGS BUNNY, PINK PANTHER, DAFFY DUCK, ROAD RUNNER, DROOPY, SCOOBY DOO.

P	I	N	K	P	A	N	T	H	E	R	R
O	J	O	C	M	N	P	O	H	U	O	E
P	I	Z	U	C	R	Z	M	C	I	A	T
E	Y	H	D	Y	O	O	X	J	X	D	S
Y	N	L	Y	O	K	L	O	E	T	R	E
E	N	E	F	I	L	M	P	R	E	U	V
S	U	G	F	U	A	I	B	R	C	N	L
C	B	H	A	A	W	U	V	Y	V	N	Y
R	S	E	D	A	T	L	O	E	B	E	S
E	G	P	T	C	L	Y	P	O	O	R	D
E	U	X	H	W	U	J	N	B	D	Y	F
Z	B	S	C	O	O	B	Y	D	O	O	L

ANSWERS

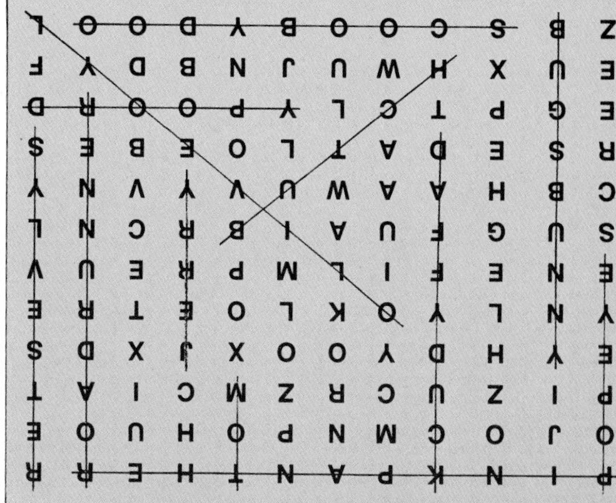

MISSING LINK
1. A Question Of Sport
2. The Pyramid Game
3. Going For Gold
4. Give Us A Clue.
5. Strike It Lucky
6. What's My Line?

ALL MIXED UP
1. Grange Hill
2. Going Live
3. Blind Date
4. Blockbusters
5. Motormouth
6. Surprise Surprise

SOAP SPOT
1. Charlie
2. Damon Grant (Simon O'Brien)
3. Alexis Carrington/ Colby/Dexter etc.
4. Patrice
5. A Country Practice
6. Braddock

IN THE FAMILY
1. Bread
2. Brookside
3. The Cosby Show
4. Family Ties
5. Dynasty
6. Home and Away

QUICK QUIZ
1. Amanda
2. The Hogan Family
3. Gordon
4. The Golden Girls
5. Top of the Pops
6. Bedrock

KIDS STUFF
1. Pat
2. Rainbow
3. Andy Pandy
4. Mr Benn
5. Play School
6. The Trumpton Firemen

Now add up your scores and check out your T.V. rating.

Over 40
Okay, square-eyes! We all know how *you* spend your time. The mystery is how you managed to find a spare ten minutes to do this quiz. You'd better get back to the box *now* — just in case you're missing something mega-brill — like Panorama!

24 - 40
Pretty average — that's you. Like most of us, you tend to watch a lot of telly — even if it's not exactly ultra interesting. It might be an idea to try to pick and choose what you watch a bit more.

11 - 25
You're probably pretty choosy about what you watch — which isn't a bad thing at all. You'll know a lot about your fav. programmes but you don't watch just *anything!* Good for you!

Minus Anything - 10
Excuse me, but you're supposed to switch on your T.V. set before you watch! You've either been staring at a black screen for years or you don't even *have* a set — in which case, why are you doing this quiz? Never mind, maybe you know a lot about crochet!

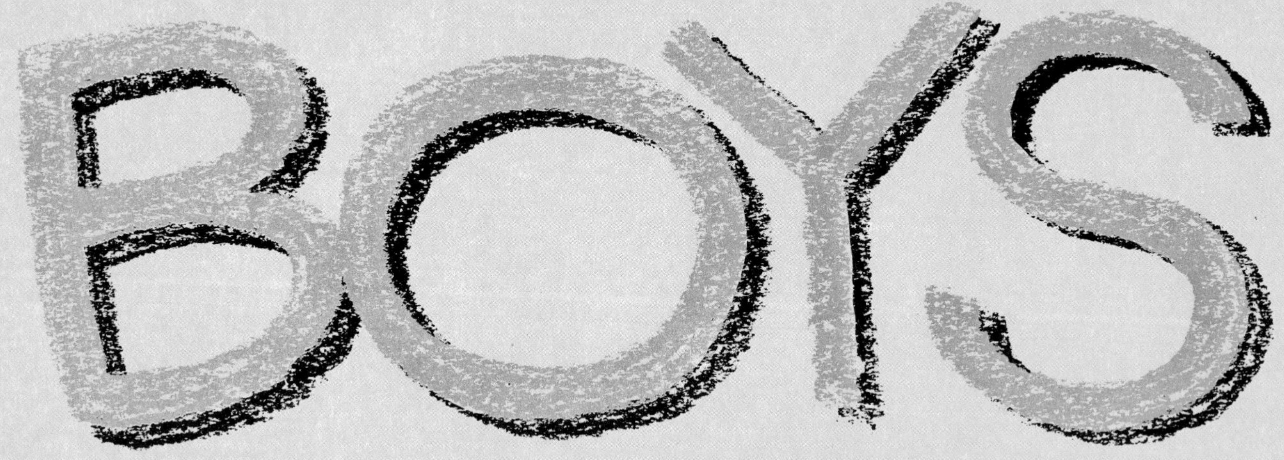

– WHY WE LOVE 'EM!

They're not all bad! Sometimes they do JUST the right thing, and then we forget why they annoy us so much!

He's off on holiday for a fortnight, and writes you a letter every day he's away.

He queues up all night to get you a ticket for a Bros concert.

He comes for tea wearing a tie, brings your mum a bunch of flowers and doesn't argue about football with your dad!

He remembered Valentine's Day.

He pretends to like Bros.

You've got the flu, your hairdryer's broken and your hair's a mess. You're wearing a pair of tatty jeans and a baggy old top — and he still thinks you look lovely.

He gives up going to watch his favourite football team for six weeks, just so's he can buy you an extra-special Christmas pressie.

He turns up for a smoochie evening — only to discover you're babysitting for your little brother. So he takes you both to the cinema instead.

It's your birthday. He says he's broke and can't take you anywhere, but would you like to come round to his place instead. You go — and discover he's planned a surprise party just for you.

He always laughs at your jokes.

You've just seen the latest Michael J. Fox movie, and you love it. And you want to see it again and again and again.
And he goes with you every time.

When you ask him what he wants for his birthday he asks for a framed photograph of you.

Your favourite pop person has gone and got hitched, leaving you in a state of depression. You've just spent the day snivelling into a hanky . . . when he presents you with a box of chocs to cheer you up.

He's given you his last Rolo.

You've pinched his favourite leather jacket to wear to a party — and he doesn't mind.

You've finally had the perm you've been talking about for yonks — and it's awful. And he doesn't say a word.

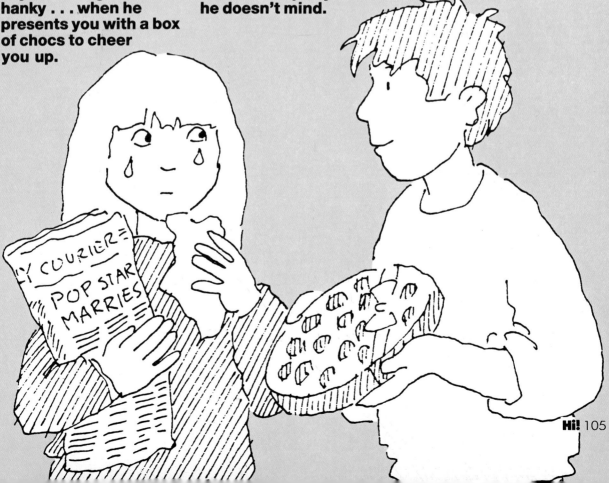

Alone!

PART 4

continued from page 84

AMANDA, WILL YOU GET UP NOW! IT'S NOT HEALTHY, MOPING AROUND THE HOUSE LIKE THIS. BESIDES, I WANT YOU TO GET SOME SHOPPING FOR ME.
OH, NO! I DON'T WANT TO GO OUT IN CASE I MEET JIM. WHY DID I EVER WRITE THAT LETTER TO KATHY, SAYING I WAS GOING OUT WITH HIM?

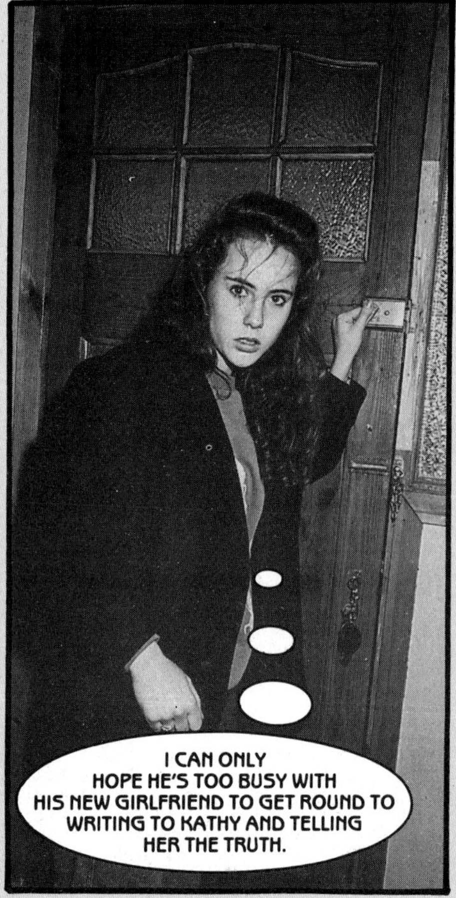

I CAN ONLY HOPE HE'S TOO BUSY WITH HIS NEW GIRLFRIEND TO GET ROUND TO WRITING TO KATHY AND TELLING HER THE TRUTH.

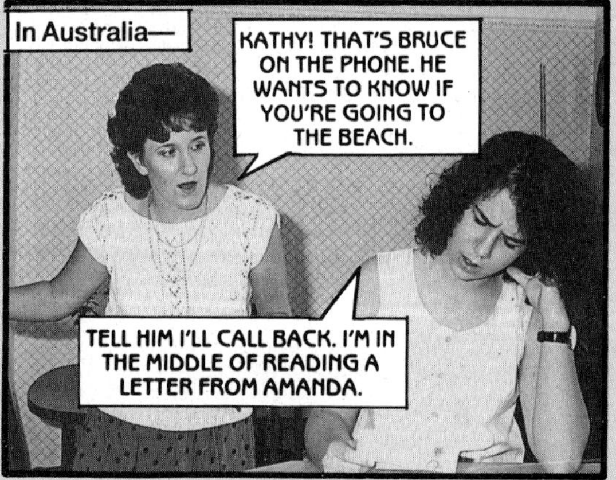

In Australia—
KATHY! THAT'S BRUCE ON THE PHONE. HE WANTS TO KNOW IF YOU'RE GOING TO THE BEACH.
TELL HIM I'LL CALL BACK. I'M IN THE MIDDLE OF READING A LETTER FROM AMANDA.

And—
MUM — HAVE A LOOK AT THIS. AMANDA SAYS SHE'S GOING OUT WITH JIM, BUT I THINK THERE'S SOMETHING FUNNY GOING ON.

WELL, IF YOU ASK ME, I'D SAY SHE'S FINE AND YOU'RE IMAGINING THINGS. BRUCE SAID TO CALL HIM IN THE NEXT TEN MINUTES OR HE'D GO WITHOUT YOU.
HUH! LET HIM! HE'S NOT AS MUCH FUN AS I THOUGHT HE WAS. BESIDES, I STILL THINK SOMETHING'S WRONG WITH AMANDA.

Back in Britain—
I DON'T USUALLY WALK THROUGH THE PARK, BUT THIS WAY, I'VE LESS CHANCE OF MEETING . . . OH, NO! IT'S JIM AND HIS GIRLFRIEND! WHAT AM I GOING TO DO?

HI, AMANDA! WHERE HAVE YOU BEEN HIDING?
AHH! SIMON AND FIONA! WHAT A FRIGHT!

CALM DOWN! WE WON'T EAT YOU. WE THOUGHT YOU'D SEEN US COMING.
WE'RE MEETING JIM AND RONA TO GO FOR A BURGER. FANCY COMING?

ER, NO — I DON'T THINK I HAVE TIME . . .
OH, PLEASE, AMANDA. I KNOW WE GOT OFF ON THE WRONG FOOT, BUT I'D STILL LIKE TO BE FRIENDS.
AND YOU AND I USED TO BE MATES. REMEMBER?

WELL, I SUPPOSE I COULD — FOR A LITTLE WHILE.
GREAT — YOU HAVEN'T MET JIM'S GIRLFRIEND RONA, HAVE YOU? SHE'S NICE — I'M SURE YOU'LL LIKE HER.

So—
HI — LOOK WHO WE RAN INTO.
AMANDA! HEY, IT'S NICE TO SEE YOU. I WAS JUST THINKING ABOUT YOU LAST NIGHT.

SO **THAT'S** WHY YOU MISSED OUR DATE. WELL I'VE HAD ENOUGH — I'M GOING HOME!
WHAT? YOU CAN'T JUST WALK OFF LIKE THAT.

But she did—
LOOKS LIKE YOU AND RONA AREN'T GETTING ON TOO WELL.
IT'S MY FAULT. I'M JUST NOT SURE IF I WANT TO GO OUT WITH HER ANY MORE — AND I SUPPOSE IT SHOWS.

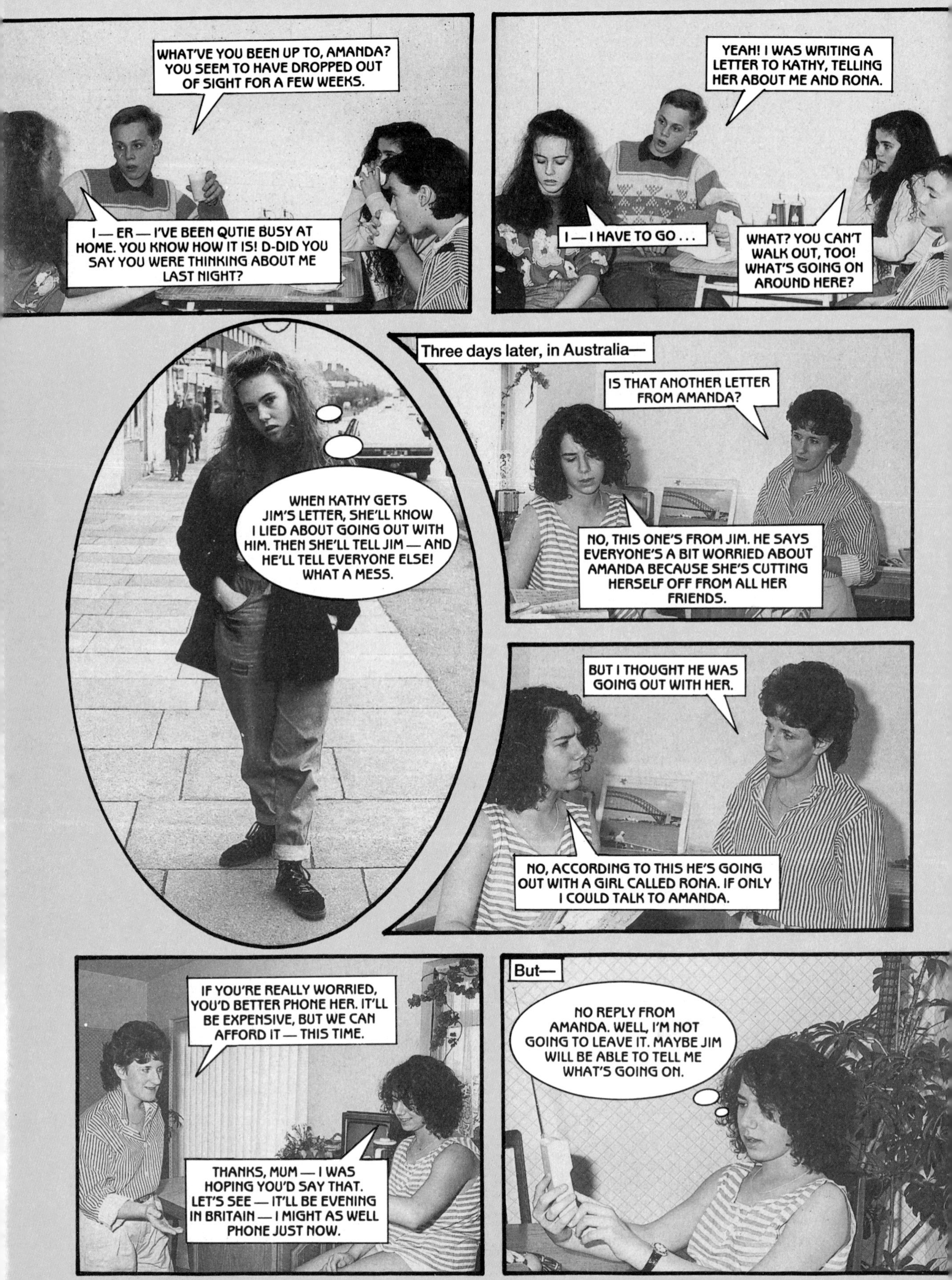

WHEN KATHY GETS JIM'S LETTER, SHE'LL KNOW I LIED ABOUT GOING OUT WITH HIM. THEN SHE'LL TELL JIM — AND HE'LL TELL EVERYONE ELSE! WHAT A MESS.

Three days later, in Australia—

IS THAT ANOTHER LETTER FROM AMANDA?

NO, THIS ONE'S FROM JIM. HE SAYS EVERYONE'S A BIT WORRIED ABOUT AMANDA BECAUSE SHE'S CUTTING HERSELF OFF FROM ALL HER FRIENDS.

BUT I THOUGHT HE WAS GOING OUT WITH HER.

NO, ACCORDING TO THIS HE'S GOING OUT WITH A GIRL CALLED RONA. IF ONLY I COULD TALK TO AMANDA.

HELLO — IS THAT MRS HENDERSON? IS JIM AT HOME? WELL, COULD YOU TELL HIM KATHY CALLED. YES, THAT'S RIGHT — KATHY FROM AUSTRALIA.

Meanwhile, at the Youth Club—
AMANDA'S MEANT TO BE COMING TONIGHT. HAS ANYONE SEEN HER?
I THINK I SPOTTED HER IN THE KITCHEN HIDING BEHIND A FRIDGE!
I GET THE DISTINCT IMPRESSION SHE'S TRYING TO AVOID US, JIM.

WHAT ABOUT RONA? IS SHE COMING?
NO — I'VE FINISHED WITH HER. SHE WAS CONVINCED I REALLY FANCIED SOMEONE ELSE.
AND IS SHE RIGHT?

OH, THERE'S AMANDA! I'LL BE RIGHT BACK — I JUST WANT TO SPEAK TO HER.
YOU'LL BE LUCKY TO CATCH HER AT THE RATE SHE'S GOING.

By the time Jim got to the door, Amanda had gone—
I KNOW I'M ACTING LIKE AN IDIOT — BUT I JUST COULDN'T FACE JIM. I BET HE AND SIMON ARE HAVING A GOOD LAUGH AT ME RIGHT NOW.

Later, when Jim got home—
WHAT ON EARTH? A PHONE MESSAGE FROM KATHY! I WONDER WHY SHE CALLED ME? MAYBE AMANDA'LL KNOW.

HELLO, AMANDA? IT'S JIM. I'VE JUST HAD A MESSAGE THAT KATHY PHONED FROM AUSTRALIA. ANY IDEA WHAT IT MIGHT BE ABOUT?
WHAT? OH, NO! I —I DON'T KNOW ANYTHING ABOUT IT. 'NIGHT, JIM.

I KNOW **EXACTLY** WHY SHE WANTS TO SPEAK TO HIM. I WONDER IF MUM WILL LET ME PHONE AUSTRALIA, SO I CAN EXPLAIN?

YOU MUST BE JOKING! DO YOU KNOW HOW MUCH THESE PHONE CALLS COST? IF YOU WANT TO SAY ANYTHING TO KATHY, YOU CAN WRITE HER A LETTER!
AW, MUM!
BY THE TIME A LETTER GETS THERE, SHE'LL HAVE PHONED JIM AGAIN — AND I'LL BE A LAUGHING STOCK.

Next day, Simon and Fiona came to visit Amanda—
OH, I — I WASN'T EXPECTING ANYONE TO CALL. WHAT D'YOU WANT?
JUST TO TALK, AMANDA. WE HARDLY EVER SEE YOU THESE DAYS.
YOU ALWAYS SEEM SO MISERABLE AND LONELY. WE THOUGHT YOU COULD DO WITH A FRIENDLY CHAT.

I SUPPOSE YOU'RE RIGHT. I HAVEN'T BEEN VERY NICE TO YOU RECENTLY, HAVE I?
IS IT JUST BECAUSE KATHY LEFT THE COUNTRY — OR IS THERE SOMETHING ELSE?
YOU CAN TELL US, AMANDA. WE REALLY **ARE** YOUR FRIENDS.

YEAH, THAT'S WHAT IT IS — I CAN'T GET USED TO LIFE WITHOUT KATHY. DON'T WORRY — I EXPECT I'LL GET OVER IT SOON.
I'D LOVE TO TELL SOMEONE WHAT'S **REALLY** BOTHERING ME — BUT I CAN'T.

Next day—
. . . SO SHE APOLOGISED FOR BEING UNFRIENDLY, AND SAID SHE WAS GETTING OVER IT NOW. BUT I'M SURE THERE'S SOMETHING ELSE BOTHERING HER.
I HATE SEEING HER SO UNHAPPY. IF ONLY I COULD THINK OF A WAY TO MAKE EVERYTHING COME RIGHT FOR HER.

Two days later—
HI, AMANDA. CAN I TALK TO YOU?
YOU'D BETTER COME IN, OH — ARE THESE FLOWERS FOR ME?

YEAH, I WAS PASSING THE FLOWER SHOP AND — OH, HECK! I BET YOU THINK I WAS WET TO BRING THEM!
OH, NO! I THINK THEY'RE **BEAUTIFUL,** JIM. NO ONE'S EVER GIVEN ME FLOWERS BEFORE. NOW, WHAT DID YOU WANT TO TALK ABOUT?

YOU'VE PROBABLY HEARD I SPLIT WITH RONA. YOU SEE, IT'S **YOU** I FANCY — BUT I NEVER DARED TO TELL YOU. I TRIED WRITING TO YOU AT THE SAME TIME I WROTE TO KATHY, BUT THEN I DIDN'T POST EITHER OF THE LETTERS.
WHAT? YOU MEAN YOU DIDN'T SEND KATHY A . . . OH, THE PHONE.

KATHY! IS THAT REALLY YOU?
I TRIED TO CALL YOU BEFORE, BUT YOU WERE OUT. I EVEN TRIED JIM'S HOUSE IN CASE YOU WERE THERE.
JIM'S HERE IF YOU WANT TO SPEAK TO HIM.
NO, BUT YOU CAN SAY HELLO FROM ME. I JUST WANTED TO TELL YOU HOW PLEASED I AM YOU TWO HAVE GOT TOGETHER.
NOT AS PLEASED AS I AM. IT'S THE BEST THING THAT'S EVER HAPPENED TO ME. IT'S ALMOST AS IF SOMEONE HAD PLANNED IT THIS WAY.
Later—
HELLO, KATHY? IT WORKED. WE'VE JUST HAD A BRILLIANT EVENING TOGETHER.
THAT'S GREAT, JIM. I'M GLAD YOU PHONED ME AND WE GOT IT ALL SORTED OUT!
MIND YOU — THERE IS STILL ONE BIG PROBLEM.
EH? WHAT'S THAT?
MY MUM! WHEN SHE SEES THE PHONE BILL SHE'S GOING TO MURDER ME!
the end

Hi!
PHILLIP SCHOFIELD
H

DRESS FOR THE OCC

● Even if you wouldn't normally be seen in a dress, it's a must if you're off to visit your gran! But dresses needn't be boring! Poppy chose one with a short skirt and bright pink top, so she could still keep in fashion. And so Gran couldn't find fault with her hair, Poppy tied it neatly back out of the way.

● Just 'cos you've nothing to do, doesn't mean to say you needn't dress for the occasion. A baggy shirt and jeans means you'll be able to lounge about in comfort — and if someone calls to say 'come out' — then a waistcoat and a neck scarf's all you need to complete your look!

ASION

SHOPPING WITH FRIENDS

IF YOU'VE SOMEWHERE TO GO, MAKE SURE YOU LOOK THE PART. THAT WAY YOU'LL FEEL GOOD, LOOK GOOD — AND WHATEVER YOU'RE UP TO WILL GO JUST RIGHT!

● A shopping trip with friends means lots of walking and lots of fun! So flat shoes are a must! You'll need to wear something you can move in — these cycling shorts are just right, and the loose jacket is easy to wear, too.

A side plait means Poppy's hair will look good all day — a splash of bright pink adds colour to her black outfit.

Smart black looks great for a special night out — jazz it up with splashes of colour! Poppy chose bright green and pink, but anything goes — try red and yellow or purple and orange.

Your hair's a great place to add colour with ribbons and scarves — give them a go!

Where's he taking you? What'll you say? What'll you do? First dates can be rather nerve-wracking, so it's important that whatever you're wearing, you'll be able to relax in it.

So put on your comfiest pair of jeans, a smart top, shoes you can walk in (!) and off you go!

Our model Poppy decided to put her hair up, so it looked neat, and that kept it out of her way, too.

BEAUTY ON A BUDGET

You don't need piles of money to look gorgeous — all you need are a few everyday ingredients and some of our money saving tips! Expensive cleansers, toners and moisturisers may seem like the answer, but if you look in your cupboard at home you could find a less expensive, but just as effective, alternative. If you want to look good, then it's important to have a good cleansing, toning and moisturising routine. Here are a few simple, low — cost recipes which you could try.

CLEANSING

1 tblsp. natural yoghurt
1 tblsp. pure lemon juice

Mix these two ingredients together and rub gently into your face. Wipe off with clean tissues or cotton wool.

TONING

A few grapes
Natural yoghurt

Cut a grape in half and rub the cut end gently over your face. Or alternatively, skin, de-pip and mash the grapes in a bowl with some natural yoghurt to make a toning mask. You'll really appreciate how good this is if you leave the mask on for ten-to-fifteen minutes, then rinse off with lukewarm water.

MOISTURISING

2 eggs
1 teasp. lemon juice
1 tblsp. glycerine and rosewater (You'll find it in Boots)
2 teasp. vegetable oil
2 beaten egg yolks
2 tblsp. water

Blend together everything except the egg yolks and water until you have a thick cream. Add the egg yolks and water a little at a time to the cream, stirring constantly.

Keep in the fridge.

Eating the correct foods also helps improve your skin's appearance.

REMEMBER — FRESH IS BEST!

Include lots of apples, oranges, bananas, carrots, broccoli, cabbage, potatoes (not chips!) etc., in your everyday diet. (Yes, all the things you hate!)

DON'T

. . . Buy fancy cotton wool balls. They're too expensive.

. . . Use toilet paper or cheap tissues on your face. It's too rough and will scratch your skin.

DO

. . . Buy large rolls of cotton wool — it's much cheaper and if you leave it in a hot place it will expand even more.

. . . Drink lots of water every day. You'll notice a tremendous difference in your complexion — especially if you cut out tea, coffee, lemonade etc.

HER ankle throbbed. Carrie winced as she tried to sit up in bed to drink her coffee. She looked down at her leg, in plaster up to her knee. Her gaze moved up to the wardrobe at the end of her bed and the new 'Next' dress hanging over its door, all pressed and ready to wear. Except she wouldn't be wearing it. Not to the school disco anyway.

Everyone was going to the school Christmas disco. It was always THE big event of the school year. Carrie had been a bit apprehensive about it all, particularly when people started discussing what they were going to wear and who they were going to go with. The first problem had been solved last Saturday night when Mum and Dad had come back from town with an early Christmas present.

"It's all you're getting, my lady, so don't go expecting anything else on Christmas day," Mum said.

"When your mother and I saw it we just couldn't resist it. It looked exactly you," Dad said, winking at Mum.

Carrie smiled through gritted teeth. Mum and Dad's idea of what was 'exactly you' was always a bit hit or miss. Visions of past Christmas presents and stripy legwarmers and flowery sweatshirt dresses flashed past and Carrie started praying it'd be the wrong size. However, this time, her mum and dad had well and truly 'hit' as far as taste was concerned. The dress was an absolutely gorgeous black creation from 'Next'. Carrie couldn't believe it and rushed to try it on. The dress had a big square neck and a fitted top.

"It's exactly like that one Aunt Debbie and I saw in her magazine, Mum," gushed Carrie straightening the skirt.

"Well, actually . . .", Mum said, blushing a bit, "we met your Aunt Debbie in the High Street. It was Debs who suggested the dress for your school dance. Well, more than suggested really," Mum giggled. "Your father and I had already got you a dressing-gown and a leather handbag, but Debbie was positive you'd hate them so your dad took them back and Debs and I went to get the dress."

Carrie gave her a big hug.

"It's brilliant, Mum. I love it." While saying all this she made a mental note to buy the biggest bar of chocolate ever as a 'thank you' for her sweet-toothed Aunt Debbie, Mum's youngest sister.

Knowing she was going to look "incredibly trendy" as well as "absolutely gorgeous" (Aunt Debbie's exclamations when Carrie tried on the dress the following day) made Carrie's confidence soar at school on Monday. However, it still didn't solve the problem of who to go with.

It wasn't actually a *huge* problem. Carrie went around with a big gang of girls and boys and they all had tickets so it wasn't as if she was going to be sitting around on her own all night. Actually, apart from Kate and Nadia, none of her friends had 'boyfriends'. But there was Gary Johnson. The new-found confidence spurred her on and she plucked up enough courage to speak to Gary during break on Tuesday.

The conversation quickly got on to that Saturday's Christmas disco. Carrie dropped loads of subtle hints about not having anyone to dance with, etc., but Gary just went red and started talking about Jamie Edwards who was hiring a white tuxedo for Saturday night.

The bell rang for the beginning of classes. Well, it was now or never . . .

"Would you like to go to the disco with me?"

"Yeah . . . okay . . . I'd love to," Gary replied. "Em, how about meeting at the Wimpy at quarter to seven?" And with that he was gone in the rush.

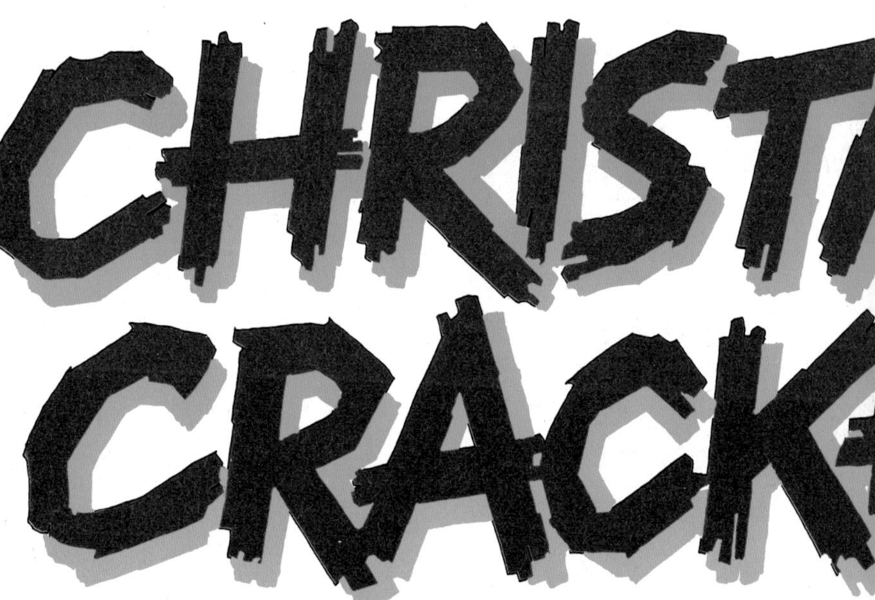

MAS

ER

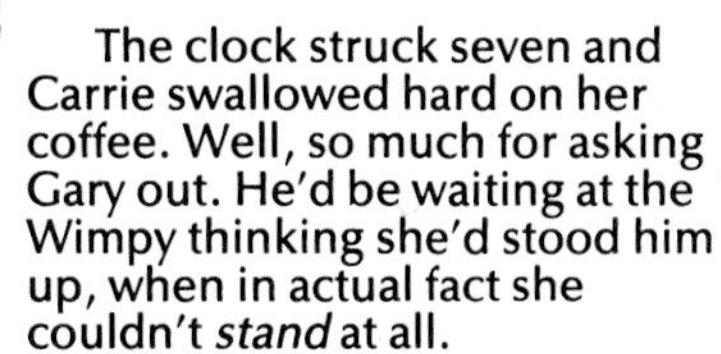

The clock struck seven and Carrie swallowed hard on her coffee. Well, so much for asking Gary out. He'd be waiting at the Wimpy thinking she'd stood him up, when in actual fact she couldn't *stand* at all.

She'd been rushing back from the hairdresser's when she'd slipped and fallen down the steps at the front door.

The x-ray showed a broken bone in her foot and about an hour and a half later Carrie was hobbling from the accident and emergency department of the Western Infirmary with her leg in plaster!

It wasn't a bad fracture, just a chip off one bone and another one cracked. Just bad enough to keep her immobile until term started again — and all the Christmas parties were over. But it wasn't *all* the parties she was bothered about — only this one.

She'd finally asked Gary Johnson out. The boy she'd secretly fancied all term. He'd said "yes"; she had the most gorgeous dress in the world, courtesy of brilliant Aunt Debbie; she'd even had her hair cut, then — wham — she'd slipped down the steps and broken her foot. Typical! Why was life so unfair?

A knock at her bedroom door made her jump.

"Hi, it's me," Aunt Debbie said as she popped her head around the door. "Your mum phoned to tell me what happened and as I was driving around to see you I just happened to be passing the Wimpy and thought, 'what the heck' . . ."

With that a sheepish-looking Gary Johnson walked in clutching a box of Milk Tray.

"Hi, how are you doing? Your auntie told me about your foot. Does it hurt?"

Carrie nodded and smiled at Aunt Debbie. She was absolutely brilliant!

"Here, I know it's no consolation, but I thought this'd cheer you up. Your aunt said you like chocolates."

Aunt Debbie's eyes twinkled and she smiled as she left the room.

"I broke my leg once and I know how boring it can be sitting around for days on end. Maybe I could come round and visit you, you know, cheer you up a bit?"

"That'd be great," Carrie smiled.

"Is this the dress you got for tonight? It's just as nice as your aunt said it was. We'll have to make sure we go somewhere nice once your foot's better so that you can wear it."

Carrie nodded, a huge grin spreading over her face.

"Well, I guess I'd better go. I'll come round tomorrow and tell you all about the disco." And with that he was gone. Carrie thought she was going to explode, she was *so* happy!

Aunt Debbie entered Carrie's room.

"Well, how did it go?" she asked, a smile twitching at the corners of her mouth.

"Brilliant, he's going to take me out once I'm better. How did you know which boy was Gary anyway? Did he look really upset?"

"Don't be so soppy. I just went around the Wimpy asking every boy who was there," Aunt Debbie laughed. "Come on then, are you going to give me a choccie or what?"

LONG HAIR'S LOVELY BUT IT CAN ALSO LOOK HORRIBLE IF YOU DON'T CARE FOR IT PROPERLY. NOTHING LOOKS WORSE THAN A HAYSTACK PERCHED ON TOP OF YOUR HEAD, SO TAKE CARE OF YOUR HAIR.

1

OVELY

MAKE sure you condition your hair well (especially if it's permed or coloured) and never brush it when it's wet. A wide toothed comb is much gentler and it's better for getting rid of tangles. Use a deep conditioner once a week and pay particular attention to the ends as they can become very dry.

Have your hair trimmed regularly to help prevent split ends and don't try to perm or colour your hair yourself. It's very easy to have a disaster with long hair when home hairdressing, as textures and condition can vary so much from the roots to the ends. So, if you don't want to end up with two inches of broken hair (a *bit* extreme perhaps, but it can happen) save up and go to a good hairdresser!

IF YOU'RE STUCK FOR STYLES, HERE'S A SELECTION TO GIVE YOU SOME IDEAS.

1.
This style is really simple. All you do is take your hair round to one side, divide it into two sections and twist them together. The front is then pinned back into a small roll and held in place with some hairspray.

2.
This style needs a bit more practice as you need to put your hair into a French plait first. To do this take a section from the top of your head at the front and a section from each side of your head and plait them together. Keep taking sections from the side as you work your way down until you reach the nape of your neck and then plait the length of hair as you would normally. Now simply tuck the plait up and wrap a scarf round it.

3.
Another easy one. All you do here is tie two sections from the sides up on to the top of your head. Then just tie the whole lot into a pony tail at the nape of your neck, and that's it!

4.
It's often quite difficult to achieve a style like this if you have very long hair, because it can just flop. The way to stop this happening is to tie your hair back into a pony tail at the nape of your neck first. Then securely pin the pony tail up on to the top of your head and back comb the ends. Spray with hairspray to hold everything in place.

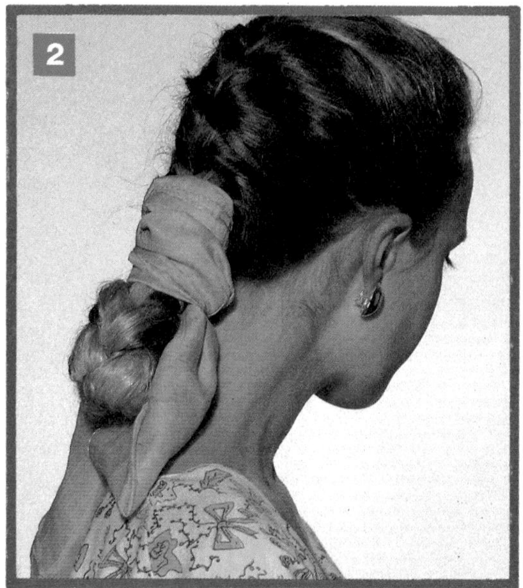

2

3

4

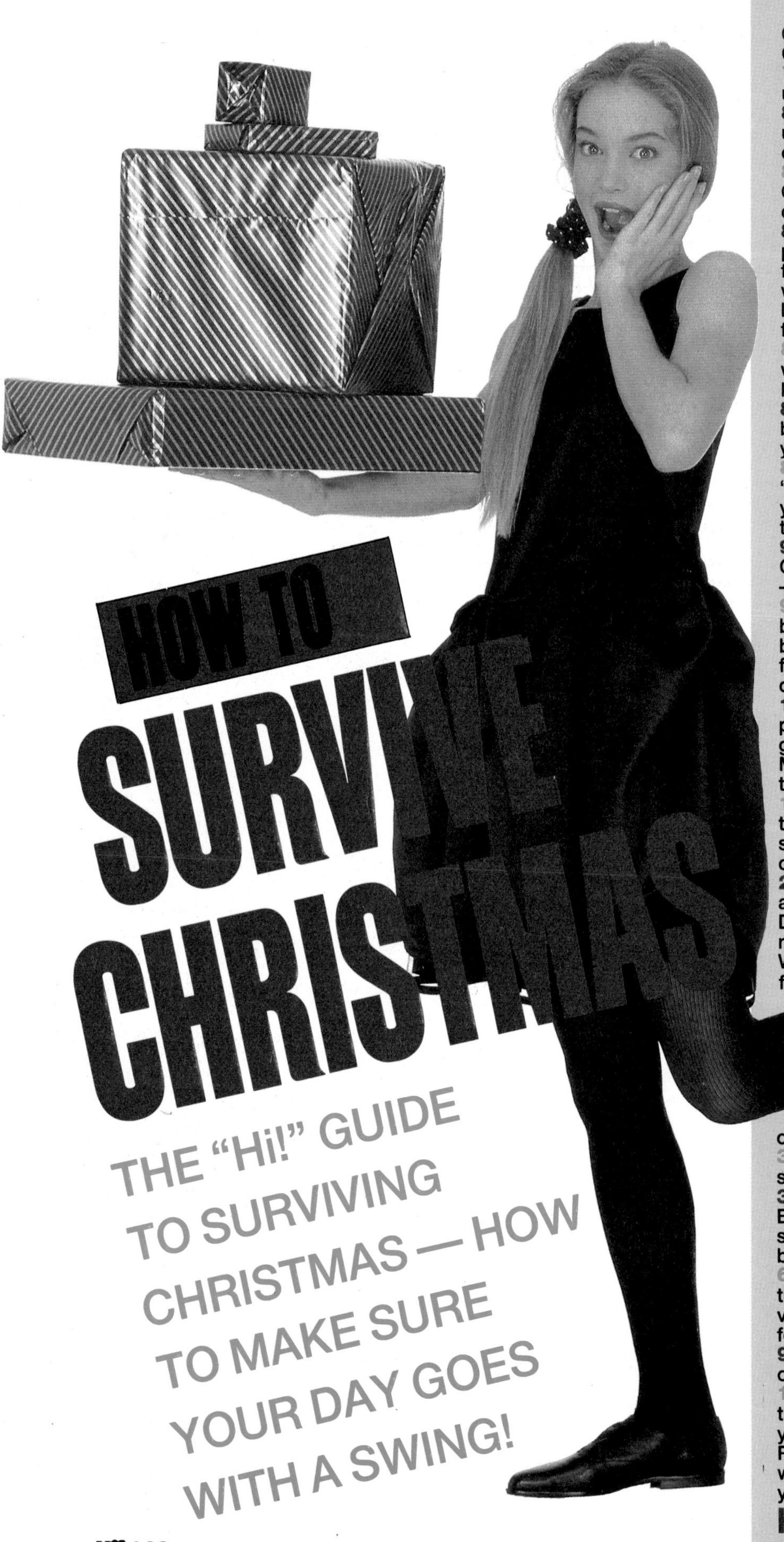

HOW TO SURVIVE CHRISTMAS

THE "Hi!" GUIDE TO SURVIVING CHRISTMAS — HOW TO MAKE SURE YOUR DAY GOES WITH A SWING!

6.30 am What? You're awake? Get back to sleep!
7.30 am Still too early . . . back under the covers with you!
8.00 am Oh, all right, you can get up now — but do it quietly — some of your family could still be asleep!
8.01 am Wish everyone a 'Merry Christmas' (everyone who's up, of course!).
8.02 am Start opening your presents. Keep a fixed grin on your face so you look pleased even when you open the rotten ones — like the baby-pink nylon nightdress from your Aunt Muriel.
8.03 am Gather up all the wrapping paper, gift tags . . . keep in Mum's good books!
8.10 am Have some breakfast before you're tempted to tuck into your selection boxes.
8.30 am Settle down with your "Hi!" annual — it'll definitely put you in a good mood for the rest of the day!
9.00 am Okay — you can have ONE thing from your selection box — and THAT'S ALL!
9.15 am Into the bathroom for a bath or shower — and use the bubble bath/ soap/ talc you got from your little sis — even if it doesn't smell too good.
10.00 am Look pleased when your parents announce that you're all going round to visit Great Aunt Matilda — and keep smiling during the visit, too!
1.00 pm Back home again — offer to help Mum/Dad in the kitchen or set the table — it could get you out of the washing-up!
2.00 pm Okay, so Mum's announced it's time for Christmas Dinner — and that means you'll miss 'Top Of The Pops'. No, she WON'T let you eat your dinner in front of the telly, so you've got two choices — miss it, or tape it!
3.20 pm If you're STILL eating — stop! You've had too much!
3.30 pm Settle down to watch the Big Film — and yes, you can have something else from your selection box.
6.00 pm Still smiling? Good, 'cos this is usually the time when various relatives descend on you for a party.
9.30 pm Are they still there? Hang on a little longer!
10.00 pm Still there? Well, "Hi!" thinks you could probably excuse yourself, and go off to bed. Remember to take some leftovers with you for a midnight feast, and your "Hi!" annual for a good read!

HAVE A GREAT CHRISTMAS!

WHAT'S IN A KISS?

Kissing's easy . . . how do we know? Well, the "Hi!" gang are experts (sort of!) so we've put together this special guide to help you lot out. Remember, practice makes perfect!

FIRST KISS

Everyone thinks their first kiss is going to be a big deal . . . until it's over, and then they wonder what the fuss was all about!

How do you know if he's going to kiss you? He'll look embarrassed, uncomfortable, inch slowly towards you, scrunch up his eyes, and open his mouth . . . actually it's much more fun than it sounds! And what do you do? Much the same, really — and if you relax, that'll help, too!

Of course, if you don't want to kiss him, then don't — it's YOUR choice!

YUCKS!

If you're planning to get into a kiss-up situation, then there are a few things to avoid . . . like garlic, onions, curry, chewing gum, chilli and cheese 'n' onion crisps! And likewise, avoid anyone who's been munching on any of that lot, too. You have been warned!

SMOOCH, SMOOCH!

Kisses come in all sorts — short and sweet or long and tender (ooh!). You can get friendly kisses or huge smackeroonie ones or ones that don't mean much at all. The best ones are from a boy you really like — the worst are slobbery ones from your Great Aunt Mary! Yuck!

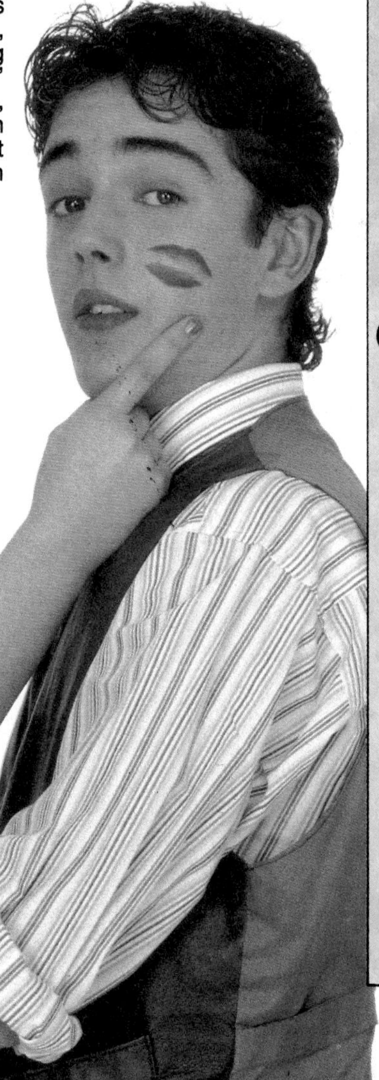

YES, PLEASE

Imagine if you could steal a kiss from any of this lot . . .
Corey Haim
Michael J. Fox
Jason Donovan
Matt 'n' Luke
Phillip Schofield
Nathan
River Pheonix
Rob Lowe
Andrew McCarthy
Marti Pellow
Rick Astley
Jon Bon Jovi

NO THANKS

. . . and imagine one from any of these . . . blee!
Curly ('Coronation Street')
Gilbert
Gary Davies
Ian Beale ('EastEnders')
Mark Curry
Timmy Mallett
Des Clark ('Neighbours')
. . . any crumblie or heavy metal singer ('cept Jon Bon Jovi)

PERFECT PAIRINGS

WE RECKONED THAT THE 'SOAPS' NEEDED A BIT MORE ROMANCE, SO WE DECIDED TO DO A BIT OF MATCHMAKING TO SEE WHAT WE COULD COME UP WITH. DO YOU THINK WE'VE FOUND THE PERFECT PAIRINGS?

HENRY RAMSEY (Neighbours) and SHARON WATTS (EastEnders)

How they meet:

Sharon's search for adventure could lead her to the land of Oz. She's walking through Errinsborough one day when a runaway lawnmower comes whizzing along the pavement and nearly knocks her flying. And who's the owner of the lawnmower — Henry!

Love at first sight?:

Not quite! Sharon would give him a right old ear-bashing at first. But then she'd calm down and see the funny side of it. And once she saw Henry's muscles, Sharon would be completely gone!

Henry, of course, as we all know, falls in love whenever he sees a pretty girl!

The first date:

They'd go to the Water Hole for some lemonade and a chat. The day would probably end with everyone in the place gathered round the piano and Sharon giving a rendition of "Yes, We Have No Bananas"!

Together forever?:

We doubt it. Sharon would be far too overpowering for Henry, and he would be far too mousey for her!

MIKE YOUNG (Neighbours) and SAMMY ROGERS (Brookside)

How they meet:

Sammy has heard the rumour that there's a new guy in town so she goes to investigate.

She can't believe her eyes when she sees Mike — and he can't believe his eyes either!

Love at first sight?:

Definitely. They both have loads to talk about together and would hit it off immediately. They might have a bit of difficulty understanding each others accents at first — but it wouldn't take them long to get it right.

The first date:

Mike would whisk Sammy off on his motor bike. They'd go to the cinema to see something romantic like 'Top Gun' and afterwards they'd have a candlelit dinner for two at the local Wimpy. (It may not sound romantic to you — but to them it would be mega!)

Together forever?:

A match made in heaven. Forget Scott and Charlene's wedding — this would be the event of the century! Imagine all the folk from Brookie and Neighbours together! And there would be the added bonus that Jason and Kylie could provide the entertainment at the reception!

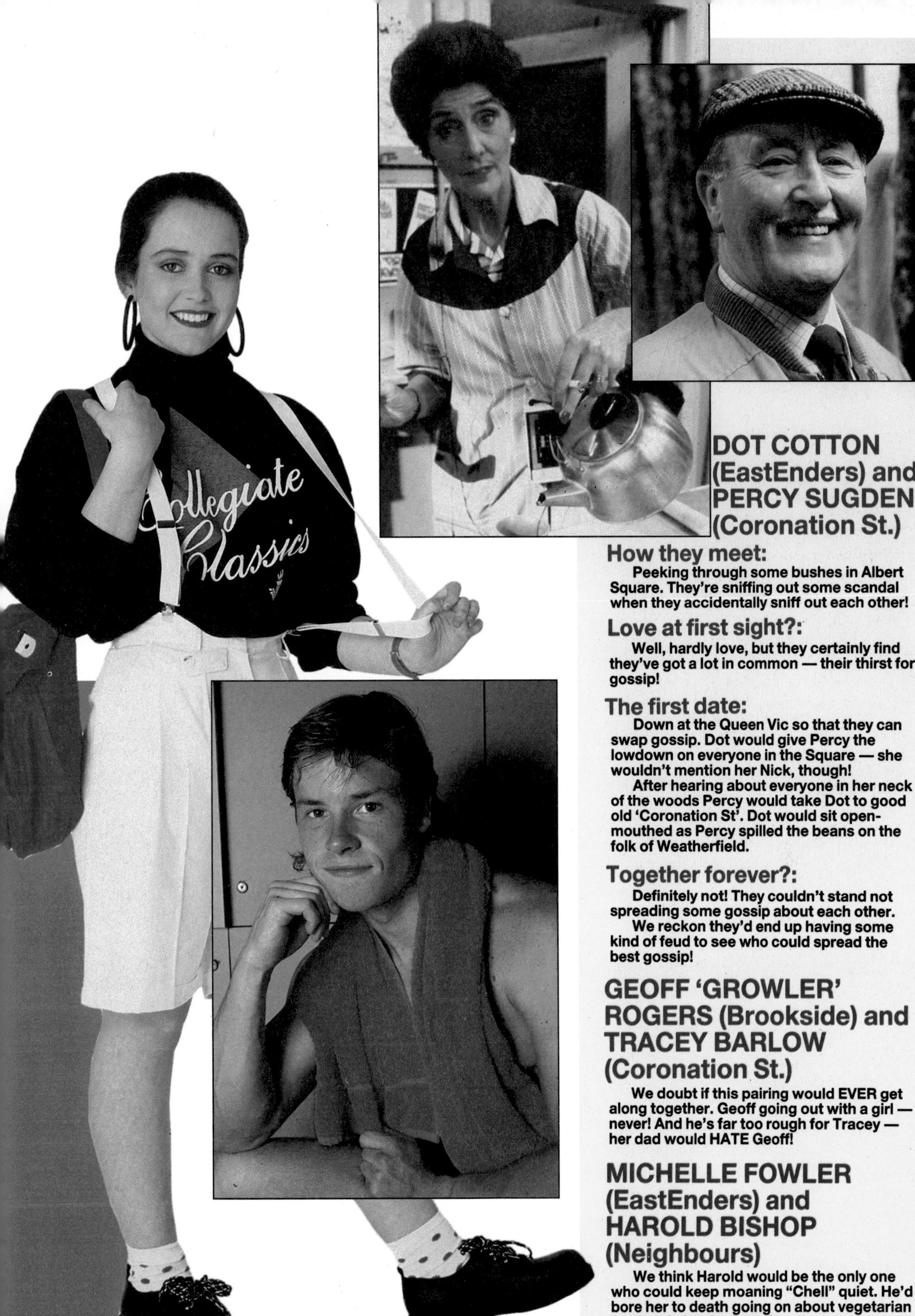

DOT COTTON (EastEnders) and PERCY SUGDEN (Coronation St.)

How they meet:

Peeking through some bushes in Albert Square. They're sniffing out some scandal when they accidentally sniff out each other!

Love at first sight?:

Well, hardly love, but they certainly find they've got a lot in common — their thirst for gossip!

The first date:

Down at the Queen Vic so that they can swap gossip. Dot would give Percy the lowdown on everyone in the Square — she wouldn't mention her Nick, though!

After hearing about everyone in her neck of the woods Percy would take Dot to good old 'Coronation St'. Dot would sit open-mouthed as Percy spilled the beans on the folk of Weatherfield.

Together forever?:

Definitely not! They couldn't stand not spreading some gossip about each other.

We reckon they'd end up having some kind of feud to see who could spread the best gossip!

GEOFF 'GROWLER' ROGERS (Brookside) and TRACEY BARLOW (Coronation St.)

We doubt if this pairing would EVER get along together. Geoff going out with a girl — never! And he's far too rough for Tracey — her dad would HATE Geoff!

MICHELLE FOWLER (EastEnders) and HAROLD BISHOP (Neighbours)

We think Harold would be the only one who could keep moaning "Chell" quiet. He'd bore her to death going on about vegetarian food and classical music.

But he's also a nice man and we think it's about time "Chell" had some good luck. If Harold could put up with Mrs Mangel we're sure he could put up with "Chell" for a while!